Where the Green Grass Grows

Where the Green Grass Grows

True (Spring and Summer) Stories from a Wisconsin Farm

(Book Number 4 in the Series)

LeAnn R. Ralph

Dedication

For my great nephew, Eli Roy Ralph, born April 18, 2006.

Your great-grandfather, Roy Arthur Ralph, would be so proud of you...

Roy Arthur Ralph
Born September 9, 1914
Died October 28, 1992

And in memory of our little black kitty cat, Nightshade, who died October 28, 2005.

You came into my life as an orphan after your mother was killed when you were only a few hours old on June 8, 1992. And over the years, you taught me much about love and about giving comfort to those you love. One day, we will find you, too, at the Rainbow Bridge.

Foreword

Several years ago, the Chippewa Valley Museum in Eau Claire, Wisconsin, published a call for pictures, documents, machinery, tools and other artifacts related to farming for a display about farm life. A small notebook from the year 1958, written in my mother's handwriting and containing a list of expenses and income for the year, was among the items I submitted to the museum.

In 2005, I received an e-mail from the museum asking permission to include part of the notebook in a traveling display that would visit different cities in the United States. The display is called "Farm Life: A Century of Change for Farm Families and Their Neighbors." The farm life exhibit's mission is to document farming, since most of the small family farms have disappeared from the landscape and are not likely to return.

My mission also is to continue documenting farm life in *Where the Green Grass Grows* with my stories of growing up on a small family dairy farm. It is a sad state of affairs that small family farms have become so scarce we must document their existence with books and museum displays before all traces of them are gone.

I would not trade my experience of growing up on a farm for anything in the world. Looking back on it, I realize we lived a simple life—a life tied to the seasons, to the animals around us, to our neighbors—and to each other.

And what could be better than that?

LeAnn R. Ralph
Colfax, Wisconsin

~ 1 ~
Easy As Flying A Kite

I bent my knees, swung my arms back, leaped forward—and landed with both feet in a puddle of water—*ker-sploosh!* Drops of water splattered high into the air and landed on the sleeve of my coat, and when I looked down at my black chore boots, the water was nearly to the first buckle. Although the sun was shining and felt warm on my head and neck and shoulders, through the thin layer of my boots, I could feel that the puddle of melted snow was icy cold.

I looked up and saw my little brown pony, Dusty, standing by the corncrib with her head hanging over the gate, waiting for me to come and see her. I had already changed out of my school clothes. Mom had given me an apple core she had been saving for Dusty and said that if I wanted to give it to my pony, by the time I was finished, the bread would be ready to take out of the oven, and then I could eat a slice of warm bread with butter and jam.

"Hi Dusty!" I shouted.

"*Weeee-heeeee-heeeee-heeeeee!*" Dusty replied.

I continued across the driveway and headed toward the silver maple tree by the gas barrel. The lawn was still covered with snow, but in places where the wind had swept some of the snow away during the winter to pile it into drifts, patches of brown grass were beginning to show. When I drew closer to the gas barrel, I stopped and looked up at the maple tree. The plump red buds were a long way from turning into leaves, but Dad said in another month or so, the trees might have tiny green leaves on them.

As I stood there looking up at the tree, a warm breeze shook the branches, and they clicked against each other, sounding like the marbles we played with at school. It was still too cold and snowy and muddy to play marbles outside, but on those days when we could not go outside for recess, our teacher let us play with them on the floor in the front of our classroom as long as we made sure to pick them all up. "The first time I step on a marble is the last time anybody plays marbles in this room. Is that understood?" our teacher had said.

I started toward Dusty's pasture once again, and a couple of puffy white clouds sailed past the granary roof. One of them looked a little like a kite with a tail trailing behind it.

"I wish I had a kite," I said to our dog, Needles, a Cocker Spaniel-Spitz mix who had jumped up from his napping spot in the sun next to the machine shed. The dog wagged his tail and watched me with his round, brown eyes. We called him Needles because when he was a tiny puppy, he had nipped my big sister's ankles while she was hanging clothes outside to dry, and she had said, 'get those needles out of here!'

"If I had a kite, then you could help me fly it," I said. Needles yawned, gathered himself, shook his fluffy cream-colored fur and wagged his tail some more.

"Wouldn't it be fun to have a kite, Dusty?" I said as I approached the gate where my pony stood, waiting patiently.

"Weeee-heeee-heeeee-heeeee!" Dusty replied, bobbing her head up and down.

"Okay, okay," I said, "here's your apple core."

I took hold of the core with both hands and snapped it in half so my pony's treat would last a little longer.

Dusty quickly snatched the first piece from my fingers, chewed, swallowed—and looked for more.

"Don't you want to say 'hi' first?" I said.

The pony bobbed her head up and down again and stretched her lips toward my hand. She chewed the second piece as quickly as the first.

"Sorry," I said. "That's all Mom had for you."

I tried to pet her soft, brown nose, but Dusty could still smell the apple on my fingers and kept nuzzling my hand.

"I don't have anything else right now," I said, turning to go back toward the house.

Needles followed me across the driveway and stopped when I stopped to look up into the blue sky.

"Doesn't a kite sound like fun, Needles?" I said.

We had finished reading a story in school a few days ago about flying kites. All you had to do was run straight into the wind, and just like that, your kite would be soaring high into the air. Much higher than the tallest trees. As high as an airplane, at least, one of the kids in the story had said.

As I walked past the gas barrel, Needles turned and went back to the machine shed. Later on, when all of the snow had melted and the weather was warmer, Needles would find somewhere else to take naps. Dad said that the machine shed, a long shiny, silver building which looked like a culvert cut in half, was a good reflector for the sun and that's why the snow had melted next to it before it had melted anywhere else on that part of the lawn.

I splashed through the puddle again on my way past the garage and then went up the porch steps one at a time so that my black rubber chore boots would leave two wet footprints on each step. I opened the porch door, kicked off my boots and headed into the kitchen. The smell of fresh, warm bread made my stomach grumble.

"Mom?" I said. "Why do people fly kites in March?"

My mother stood by the cupboard, holding onto a pastry brush with her right hand and the countertop with her left. Because of the polio that had happened a long time before I was born, my mother always held onto something with one hand to help her keep her balance.

"Why do people fly kites in March? What kind of a question is that?" she asked.

"We read a story in school about kites, and the kids in the story said March was the only time they could fly kites," I said.

"Well, March is not the *only* month you can fly kites," Mom said. "But people fly kites in March because it's the windiest month."

She dipped the little brush with the silver handle into a can of shortening and dabbed it on one of the loaves of hot bread. Mom said putting shortening on the bread when it was hot helped to keep the crust from drying out.

"Or usually March is the windiest month," she continued. "And that's what you need to fly kites is wind."

"But we have windy days in other months, too," I pointed out.

Mom dipped the brush into the shortening again. "Well, yes, you're right," she said. "But March seems to be more windy, as a rule."

"Why?"

My mother made one final swipe with the brush and then moved onto the next loaf. In a little while she would dump the loaves out of their pans, and I could hardly wait to eat a hot crust of bread with butter and homemade strawberry jam.

"I don't know *why* March is so windy," she said. "I guess April is, too, sometimes. I suppose it's related to weather conditions during the spring. Warm and cold air currents. Things like that."

She reached up to push back a lock of hair that had fallen out of place. My mother wore her dark curly hair combed back from her forehead. Mom's hair was naturally curly. She never put rollers in it or used home permanents. Sometimes my big sister used home permanents, and the smell was awful. A sweet and sour smell that made my eyes water and caused my nose to feel hot and prickly if I stood too close.

"What does warm and cold air have to do with wind?" I said.

"You know how some days in March it feels like spring is definitely here and then the next day it feels like it's still winter?" Mom asked.

"And when it feels like winter, how you think it's never going to be spring?" I replied.

My mother smiled. "Yes, that's exactly what I mean. The temperature we feel on the ground is what's going on up in the air. You've heard about March coming in like a lamb and going out like a lion, or coming in like a lion and going out like a lamb. That's one way of saying the weather is unsettled in March, and when the weather is unsettled, that means it's going to be windy."

"And wind is what you need to fly kites!" I said.

"Right," she said.

"Did you ever fly a kite?"

My mother shook her head as she picked up a hot pad. "I think Loretta and Ingman might have, though."

"In March?"

"I don't remember when, but I suppose it might have been March."

My big brother, Ingman, is twenty-one years older than me, and my sister, Loretta is nineteen years older. Mom, who had walked with crutches for as long as I had known her, had been stricken with polio and partially paralyzed in both legs when she was twenty-six years old. After the polio, the doctors said she would never have more children. I was born sixteen years later, when Mom was forty-two and Dad was forty-four.

My mother reached for the first loaf of bread and turned it out of the pan. "Do you want the crust?" she asked. "Oh, never mind. That's a silly question, isn't it."

During the following days, the more I thought about it, the more I wanted to fly a kite—in March—the windiest month of all. Just like the kids in my story. And maybe even like my brother and sister.

But first I had to figure out a way to get a kite. I had no idea how much a kite would cost, so I did not know whether I had enough money in my tea canister.

Sometimes when Mom asked me to do a cleaning job she could not do herself, and which she did not think Loretta should have to do when she was home on the weekend—such as sweeping the cobwebs off the basement ceiling—she would pay me fifty cents or a dollar. Then she would tell me to put the money in my tea canister so that when I wanted to buy something for myself—a candy bar, or a new brush for Dusty, or a new book to read—I would have enough money. Maybe if I asked my sister she would check on the prices for me at the dime store in the city where she worked. I had already asked Dad to check at the two hardware stores in town, but they didn't have any kites.

I could not ask Loretta right away, though, because she had not yet moved home from the apartment where she lived during the winter. My sister worked as an assistant bookkeeper for the electric cooperative that supplied electricity to our farm and to many rural areas in our county. She would rather not drive thirty miles round-trip every day on snowy, icy roads, so she rented an apartment, lived there during the week and came home on weekends.

As it turned out, I never got a chance to ask Loretta about checking on prices because the next Friday evening, my sister came home with a big, white package.

"What's that?" I asked, eyeing the paper bag that said *Kresge's* on it.

"Guess," my sister said, setting it on the table.

"Oh, Loretta," my mother said, "you shouldn't spoil her like that."

"But what is it?" I asked.

Loretta reached into the bag and pulled out a smaller plastic bag.

"Here," she said, holding it toward me.

A single word stood out on the label.

"This is a kite?" I said. "It doesn't look like one."

"It's folded up," my sister replied. "You have to take it out and unroll it."

So I did.

And, oh, it was *beautiful*. Bright blue and sparkling red with white trim. And red, white and blue tail streamers, too.

"How's it going to fly, though?" I asked, waving the limp plastic back and forth.

"You have to use these," Loretta explained. She fished around in the plastic bag and pulled out several small metal rods. "They fit into the back," she said, taking the kite from me to push the pieces into the sleeves around the edge.

And just like that, the kite looked exactly like a kite.

"Now all you have to do is wish for a windy day," my sister said. "Doesn't seem like we've had too many of those yet this year."

I thought back over the past few weeks and realized she was right. So far, we hadn't had any *really* windy days. Sometimes in March, the wind blew so hard I could barely walk up the hill after getting off the school bus.

"Just wait," Mom said. "It'll be windy. You'll see."

"Are you sure?" I asked.

Mom laughed. "I'm sure."

So I waited.

And waited.

And then waited some more.

"I thought March was supposed to be windy," I complained to my mother almost a week later. When I had walked up the hill a few minutes ago, the sky was cloudy and the air was as still as one of our barn cats while it waited for a mouse to come out from behind the feed box in the barn.

"Well—" Mom said, turning to look out the big picture window in the living room, "March usually is windy. Just not this year, I guess."

"But *when* will it be windy?"

"Soon, I would imagine. You must learn to be more patient," my mother said.

When I woke up Saturday morning, looked out the upstairs window and saw puffy white clouds chasing each other across a blue sky, I knew my windy day had arrived. Clouds only moved across the sky like that when it was very windy. I slipped on an old pair of pants, pulled a sweatshirt over my head and hurried downstairs. Loretta was in the basement, sorting laundry and putting in the first load to wash.

My sister always got up early on Saturday morning to start the laundry. Mom was sitting by the table with a cup of coffee.

"Looks like it's a windy day," she said.

"Windy enough to fly a kite!" I replied. "Yipeeeeee!"

I went out to the porch and put on my coat, chore boots, a hat and mittens. I could hardly wait to fly my kite, but first I would have to help Dad with the morning milking. When I pushed open the porch door, the wind tried to slam it in my face. I leaned into the door, squeezed around the edge, and with tears trickling down my cheeks from the cold, fierce wind, made my way out to the barn. As soon as I moved past the garage, the barn blocked most of the wind. I could still hear the wind roaring through the trees and whistling around the barn roof, though. With a feeling of relief because I knew it would be much warmer in the barn, I pulled open the door and went inside.

"Windy enough for you?" Dad asked as I walked down the barn aisle toward him.

"Oh, yes, Daddy!" I said, taking off my mittens and reaching up to wipe the tears out of my eyes.

A while later, after we had finished milking and had fed the calves and had given the cows more hay, Dad and I headed back to the house together.

"Hasn't been this windy in a long time," Dad said, reaching up to keep his cap from blowing away. "It's gotta be thirty miles an hour, if not forty."

"Good," I said.

"Might be a little too windy to fly your kite," he said.

"How could it be *too* windy to fly a kite?" I asked.

"This kind of wind might make it hard to hold onto it," he said.

"If I'm strong enough to carry a pail of milk, I can hold onto my kite," I said.

Dad shrugged. "Maybe so," he said as he started up the porch steps.

When my father and I had washed up and were sitting by the table, I quickly poured a bowl of cereal and buttered a slice of toast.

Ingman had come home from working the night shift at the creamery a little while ago. I knew that my big brother would eat breakfast and then he would sleep for most of the day so he could work the night shift again. He was still dressed in the white pants and white shirt that he wore to work. As I set the pitcher of milk in the middle of the table again, he caught my eye and grinned.

"I bet I know what you're going to do after breakfast," he said. "I bet you're going to...do your homework!"

I shook my head and shoveled a spoonful of cereal into my mouth.

"Then I bet you're going to...clean the house!"

I shook my head again.

"Hmmmm," he said. "Could it be that you're going to...fly your kite?"

"Either that, or the kite is going to fly away with her," Dad muttered.

"What?" I said.

"He said," Mom explained, "that maybe the kite is going to fly away with you."

I looked at Dad. He shook his head and pursed his lips, so I knew he was making a joke.

I finished my cereal, hastily chewed my last bite of toast, and then I was ready to go.

"Mom? May I be excused now?" I asked. "Please?"

My mother sighed as she set down her coffee cup.

Loretta reached out to ruffle my bangs. "Better hurry up, before the wind dies down."

"I don't think you have to worry about that," Dad said. "I think it's going to be windy like this all day."

"Can I, Mom? I mean—may I *please* be excused?"

My mother nodded. "Yes, you may be excused," she said.

Ever since Loretta had brought the kite home, it had been ready and waiting in the porch. I put my hat, coat, boots and mittens on again, picked up my kite and stepped out of the house. As I struggled to hold onto the kite, the wind blew against it and nearly lifted it out of my grasp. I grabbed the kite with both hands and headed down the concrete steps. Needles, who had been curled up by the garage out of the wind, came to meet me, his tail going in circles.

The directions on the package said to hold the kite behind you and then run into the wind while letting out the string. And just like that, you would be flying your very own kite.

Needles followed me to the edge of the blacktop and sat down. I took hold of the kite in my right hand and the string in my left, held the kite behind me, and took off running across the driveway toward the barn.

A sudden jolt brought me up short—
SPLAT!!
I turned around to see what had happened.
Instead of soaring into the bright blue sky with puffy white clouds, my kite was laying flat on the ground.
I walked back, picked up the kite, returned to the edge of the driveway where I had started, took the kite in my right hand and the string in my left and tried it again...
Ker-THUNK!
The first two times I had held the kite in my right hand and the string in my left. Maybe I should try it the other way around.
Once again, I went back to the edge of the driveway, but now I took the string in my right hand and held the kite in my left. I ran across the driveway toward the barn, letting out string as I went.
Ka-plop.
When I turned around to see what had happened to my kite this time, I discovered it had landed on a small patch of grainy snow next to the pump house. Or what Mom and Dad called the pump house. The pump house was only as tall as me—not a 'house' really—but more like a big wooden box with a slanted roof that protected the pump from the wind and the rain and the snow.
As I returned to the edge of the blacktop, I saw that Needles had given up on watching me and had curled up by the garage again, his nose buried in the tip of his bushy cream-colored tail.
I drew a deep breath, took the kite in one hand and the string in the other and tried again.
And then again.
And yet again
But each time, the kite ended up on the ground.
As I stood there trying to figure out what I was doing wrong, I heard the porch door slam shut. I looked up and saw my brother coming down the steps.
"Want me to try?" Ingman asked, zipping his coat as he walked toward me. "It looks like you're having a little trouble."
Oh, great. I had not considered that Mom and Dad and Loretta and Ingman were probably watching me from the kitchen window.
"Yeah, you can try it," I said. "I'm not having any luck."
Ingman took the kite, held it behind him, started running toward the barn—and in seconds, the kite was soaring high overhead.

Much higher than the barn roof.

Almost as high, I imagined, as an airplane would fly.

I watched as the kite swooped and sailed in the brisk March wind, red, white and blue streamers fluttering wildly behind it.

"Here," Ingman said, holding out the bundle of string.

"No, you keep it. Then you can show me what to do," I said.

Ingman grinned and then turned his attention upward again as he unwound a little more string.

"But how did you *do* that?" I asked.

"Flying a kite is easy. There's nothing to it," Ingman replied, glancing at me. "You've just got to hold it behind you, start running and let out string as the wind takes it."

Right.

Nothing to it at all.

My big brother smiled again. "I suppose it might have something to do with me being a little taller than you are, though."

"Why does it make any difference that you're taller?" I asked.

"Because that means there's more room between me and the ground, *and* between the kite and the ground, so the wind has a better chance to catch hold of it."

I looked at Ingman.

Looked up at the kite.

"Do you really think that's why I couldn't get it to fly?" I said.

My brother nodded as he held out the bundle of string again. "Here, I'll show you what to do. It's not that hard."

I reached for the string.

"There," Ingman said. "Now you're flying the kite."

I had always wondered what people meant when they said something was 'as easy as flying a kite.' And as I held the string, I could see that *flying* the kite was easy.

It was getting the kite up into the air that was the hard part.

"This is fun!" I said. The string tugged and danced against my mittened hands as the kite fluttered high overhead.

My brother watched for a few minutes. "I think I've got to get some sleep pretty soon. If I don't, I won't be able to go to work tonight," he said. "Want me to show you how to get it down again?"

I handed the spindle to my brother. Slowly he began winding up the string. "You just take it in a little bit at a time," he said. "Here, you try it."

Winding up the string, I discovered, was not quite as easy as it looked. But slowly, bit by bit, the kite came down from the sky.

"When it gets to a certain point, it's probably going to fall the rest of the way," Ingman said.

And sure enough, it did.

I picked up the kite, and together, Ingman and I walked back to the house. The wind was at our backs, and an unexpected gust pushed hard against me and nearly tore the kite from my hands.

"It's probably a little too windy to fly your kite today, anyway," Ingman said as we went into the porch. "I think it would be easier for you to fly it by yourself if it wasn't so windy."

I set the kite in the corner of the porch behind the wood box. With such a cold wind blowing today, my mother had started a fire in the stove in the living room and would most likely keep it burning all day. The wood box was nearly empty and part of my morning chores today would be to carry in more wood.

"Was it fun?" Mom asked when I walked into the kitchen.

"As much fun as you thought it would be?" Loretta inquired.

"Oh, yes," I said. "It was tons of fun."

"Kite didn't fly away with you, I see," Dad said.

"I stood on her toes so she'd stay on the ground," Ingman said.

"You did not!" I said.

I turned to look at the light yellow Farmer's Union calendar hanging on the kitchen wall. March still had a couple of days left. Which meant that I still had a couple of days to fly my kite in the windiest month of all. Just like the kids in the story we had read at school.

"I wish I could write a story about flying kites," I said.

"What?" Dad asked.

"Why?" Loretta said.

"How come?" Ingman wondered.

"Oh, I bet I know," Mom said. "She read a story in school about flying kites."

My mother turned to look at me. "Well, who knows? Maybe you will someday."

"Do you think so?" I said.
Mom shrugged. "I guess anything is possible, isn't it."

~ 2 ~
Flat as a Pancake

The moment Loretta opened the door to the kitchen, I was waiting. It was five o'clock Friday evening, and my big sister had come home for the weekend. In a few weeks, after Easter, she would give up the apartment she had rented for the winter in the city where she worked and would move home to the farm.

"Guess what?" I said as Loretta set her purse on the table.

"What?" my sister asked.

"We're going to make Easter bonnets in school on Monday!" I said.

At least once before Easter, my big sister would sing the 'Easter bonnet song'—the one that went, *"In your Easter bonnet, with all the frills upon it, you'll be the grandest lady in the Easter Parade. . .oh, I could write a sonnet about your Easter bonnet and of the girl I'm taking to the Easter Parade."*

I had seen many ladies wearing hats on Sundays at the little white church a half mile from our farm, but Mom said that those hats were not at all like the Easter bonnets in the movie called *Easter Parade*, which is where the song came from. A proper Easter bonnet, Mom said, would have a wide, swooping brim, long colorful ribbons, flowers and maybe even a large feather waving from the top.

"You're going to make Easter bonnets!" Loretta exclaimed.

My mother heaved a deep sigh and drummed her fingers against the kitchen table. "I told her not to get her hopes up," she said to Loretta. "But she thinks they are going to make regular hats out of wool or felt or straw or some such thing."

"We *are*!" I said. "That's what my teacher said—that we are going to make Easter bonnets."

Mom looked at me and shook her head. "In the first place, you would need sewing machines to make regular hats. And in the second place, someone who makes hats has spent years learning how to do it."

"But—"

"You can't tell me," my mother continued, "that your teacher is going to sew hats for every girl in class."

I shook my head. "No, *we* are making the Easter bonnets—real Easter bonnets."

"Impossible," Mom said.

"It is not impossible," I said. "We're making Easter bonnets!"

"No, you're not—not real hats, you aren't."

"Yes we are!"

My sister cleared her throat. "All right. Everybody calm down."

Mom and I turned to look at Loretta.

"I'm sure that no matter what the Easter bonnets are made out of, they will be pretty," my sister said.

"We *are* making real Easter bonnets. You'll see," I said.

"Well, maybe you could wear yours to church on Easter then," Loretta said.

My big sister wore hats to church sometimes, and so did Mom. A couple of times when we went shopping for a new dress for Easter, my sister had tried to talk me into getting a hat. The one I remembered best had been round and white and made out of something that looked like stiff gauze and had a long navy blue ribbon tied around it that hung over the back. It didn't look at all like Mom or Loretta's hats.

As for the new dress my mother insisted that I wear to church every year for Easter, personally, I would have preferred wearing pants. You could move around better in pants. I wore pants when I rode my pony, Dusty. And when I helped Dad with the milking. And when I fed the calves. And when I drove the tractor to bale hay in the summer. So why did I have to wear a dress for Easter? Although this year, it wasn't a dress, it was a skirt and a blouse. Light blue. And instead of white leotards with black shiny shoes, Loretta said white anklets with lace around the top would work just as well.

I would still rather wear pants.

"I'm telling you—you are *not* going to be making real hats," Mom said.

"We are too."

"You are not."

"Are too."

"You are not."

"Are too."

"You are *not*. And that's that."

If Mom ended something with 'and that's that'—I knew the discussion was finished. But it didn't stop me from thinking about the Easter bonnets, and when my teacher announced on Monday after lunch that we were ready to start our project, I was could hardly wait to begin.

"The first part will be the base," my teacher explained as she opened the door of her closet.

When she turned around, she was holding a stack of paper plates.

Paper plates?

Why was she holding a stack of white paper plates?

"Before you do anything else you must color the plate, so get out your crayons," the teacher continued. "Color both sides of the plate. And choose any color you like. It doesn't have to be all one color, either."

My mouth dropped open and snapped shut. I wanted to say something, except I did not know what to say. The teacher could not possibly mean that we were going to make Easter bonnets out of paper plates...could she? I sat by my desk without moving for at least a minute. Then I leaned forward.

"We're not making real Easter bonnets, you know," I whispered to the girl sitting in front me. "Real Easter bonnets are not made out of paper plates."

The girl selected a crayon and glanced back at me.

"How do you know real Easter bonnets aren't made this way? And what's wrong with making Easter bonnets like this?"

"Because they won't be real Easter bonnets!" I said.

All around me, the other girls had started coloring their plates, and I noticed that the teacher was staring in my direction and frowning.

I sat back and slowly reached into the desk for my box of crayons.

The boys in our class, instead of making Easter bonnets, were making stovepipe hats out of black construction paper. As I pulled the box of crayons out of my desk, I thought about raising my hand to ask if I could make a stovepipe hat. A hat made out of construction paper would be much better than an Easter bonnet made out of a paper plate.

The longer I thought about asking if I could make a stovepipe hat, however, the more convinced I became that the teacher would never let me do it.

Reluctantly, I opened the box of crayons. What color did I want? That light green was kind of nice, but you had to press hard to make it show up.

Yellow? Baby chicks were yellow. And so were those marshmallow chicks that I found in my Easter basket every year—but I wasn't crazy about yellow. Yellow was Mom's favorite color. Not mine.

Blue? Yes, blue was a lovely color. But which blue? There was green-blue and light-blue, cornflower-blue and violet-blue, blue-gray...

"Is something wrong?" the teacher asked, stopping by my desk. "Why haven't you started coloring your plate?"

I swallowed hard and looked up from my crayon box.

"Ummm...Nothing's wrong. I'm just trying to pick a good color."

"Well," the teacher said, "don't take all afternoon. Choose something and get started. Otherwise you'll end up too far behind."

I pulled the green-blue out of my crayon box, but then I changed my mind, put it back and reached for the violet-blue. Although it was not exactly the color of the violets that bloomed on the hill behind the barn in May, it was still a nice color.

I began on one edge and worked my way toward the middle. Then I stopped and glanced to my left and to my right. The other girls were concentrating so hard that their noses were almost pressed against the paper plates. How they could be so busy coloring? Reading a story or working on a science experiment would have been one thing. But coloring?

"I'm going to bring around some Easter grass," the teacher said after a while. "When you're done coloring, raise your hand, and I'll dab some glue on your plate."

The only place I had ever seen Easter grass was in the basket Loretta hid somewhere around the house before we went to church Easter morning. Easter grass was supposed to be in Easter baskets filled with chocolate eggs and chocolate bunnies and jellybeans and malted milk eggs—not on Easter bonnets.

"After you glue on the grass, we will start decorating," the teacher added.

As I waited for the Easter grass and the glue, I had a dreadful thought: what was I going to tell my mother? She had been right, after all. We were not making real Easter bonnets.

When the plates were finally colored and the grass had been glued in place, the teacher handed out small pieces of tag board with traced patterns of a bunny, an egg and a flower.

"Color these however you want," the teacher instructed. "And be sure to color the back, too, before you cut them out. When you've got them colored, then I'll help you staple them on top of your bonnets."

Each picture had a narrow tab on the bottom.

"Should we cut out that square part on the bottom?" asked another girl.

"Yes," said the teacher. "That's how we're going to staple it on."

After I had finished coloring the flower, the bunny and the Easter egg, and had cut them out and had folded the tabs on the bottom, I raised my hand. The teacher came over and stapled them onto the paper plate. When she had gone to another girl who had raised her hand, I turned to look at the big black and white clock on the wall next to the door and saw that it was almost time for recess.

"We'll let the glue dry until after recess, and then we'll put ribbons on," the teacher explained."

"Ribbons!" exclaimed the girl who sat in front of me. "I can hardly wait to see what colors we get!"

"Me, too!" said another girl.

"I hope we get pink!" said a third.

I leaned forward to talk to the girl in front of me. "I hope we get real ribbons," I said.

The girl turned around to look at me. "Real ribbons? What other kind of ribbon is there?"

"You know," I said, "*real* ribbons."

She shook her head and turned around.

I saw all kinds of ribbon when I went to the fabric store with my big sister: wide ribbon, narrow ribbon, velvet ribbon, some that looked like gauze and some that looked like lace. I thought about trying to explain it to the girl in front of me but then decided not to. The teacher was looking in my direction again and frowning.

After we came back inside from recess, I soon found out that the teacher's idea of ribbons was very different from mine. Instead of wide velvet ribbon, it turned out to be the narrow ribbed kind of ribbon that you tied around gifts and could curl with a scissors.

Before recess, the boys had finished their stovepipe hats, and as the rest of us put curly ribbon on the paper plates, the boys played a game at the back of the classroom. Their occasional shouts of laughter made me wish I could be playing a game, too.

"I want the girls to try on their Easter bonnets now so we can all see what they look like," the teacher said.

What they *look* like?

No matter how much we colored and no matter how much Easter grass or how many rabbits or flowers or Easter eggs or curly ribbons were stapled to the top—they were still paper plates. I didn't want to stand out from the rest of the girls, though, so I put the paper plate on my head and tied the ribbons under my chin.

"May we go to the rest room so we can look in the mirror?" one girl asked.

"Oh, yes, could we?" several other girls said.

The teacher thought about the request. "Yes, you may. As long as you go quietly in the hall and don't talk above a whisper. The other classes are still working, and I don't want you to disturb them."

"Come on," said the girl in front of me. "Let's go!"

I stood up and followed the rest of the girls. When I reached the door, I stopped and looked both ways. The hall was empty—except for the other girls from my class. Keeping my head down, I hurried to catch up with the rest of them, and with a sense of relief, I slipped into the girls' bathroom. No one else had seen me.

"Oooooo—it's so pretty," one girl gushed as she gazed at herself in the mirror.

"It's the prettiest Easter bonnet I've ever had!" another girl exclaimed.

"I love hats," said another girl.

Finally, when it seemed that I couldn't avoid it any longer, I looked in the mirror. Strapped to my head was the violet-blue paper plate with curly ribbons trailing down the back—purple curly ribbons because I figured purple was better than pink.

"I'm going to wear mine home!" one girl said, turning this way and that so she could admire her reflection in the mirror.

"Me, too!" said another.

Once we returned to the classroom, I could hardly wait to untie the ribbons and put the colored paper plate on my desk.

"How many of you are going to wear your Easter bonnets home?" the teacher asked.

Most of the girls raised their hands, but a few students, including me, did not.

"I have some paper bags for those of you who do not want to wear your Easter bonnets home," the teacher said.

I happily accepted one of the paper grocery bags, put the violet-blue paper plate in the bottom and folded down the top.

Unfortunately, I still had no idea what I was going to tell my mother, and later on, during the long bus ride home, I wondered if I could hide the paper bag somewhere before I got to the house.

Three minutes of thinking about the problem convinced me there was no place to hide the paper bag, with the pasture on one side of the driveway and the lawn on the other. Of course, the plum bushes growing in the fenceline by Dusty's pasture were a possibility, except that I would have to wade through what was left of the snow and climb through the ditch where the spring ran to get to the plum bushes.

A little while later, the school bus stopped by our mailbox. I climbed down the steps, the paper bag clutched in my right hand, and as the bus backed out of the driveway, I began to trudge up the hill. At the top of the driveway, I turned toward the house just as Dad came out of the porch door. During the winter and early spring, when there was no fieldwork to do, my father sometimes went into the house for an afternoon coffee break before feeding the cows.

"What's in the grocery bag?" he asked.

"Well, it's, ahhhhhhh...it's an Easter bonnet. Sort of," I replied.

"An Easter bonnet?" Dad said.

"We made them in school," I said. "It's not really an Easter bonnet, though. It's a paper plate."

I reached into the bag and pulled out the violet-blue paper plate.

"Hmmm," Dad said. "It's sort of the color of the violets on the Bluff in the spring."

Long before I was born, the big wooded hill behind the barn had been called the Bluff. And every spring, an open spot halfway up was blue with wild violets. The Bluff was so blue with violets that I could see them when the bus came over the first hill by the church.

"Well, I've got to feed the cows before we can eat supper," Dad said. He threw a quick wink in my direction and headed off toward the barn.

I put the paper plate back in the grocery bag. When I opened the door leading into the kitchen a minute later, my mother was sitting by the kitchen table.

"Where's your Easter bonnet? Is it in the grocery bag?" she asked.

"Yes," I said, setting the paper bag on the kitchen table.

I took off my coat, hung it in the hall closet and sat down on one of the kitchen chairs.

I looked at Mom—and she looked at me.

"Aren't you going to show me your Easter bonnet?" my mother asked at last.

"Do I have to?" I said.

"Well, of course you don't *have* to," Mom said. "But I *would* like to see it."

I unrolled the top of the paper sack and reached down inside.

"It's not really an Easter bonnet. It's a paper plate," I said.

I set the colored paper plate on the table, and all at once, my throat felt tight.

"Mom!" I said. "It's not an Easter bonnet. It's a *paper plate...*"

My mother sighed. "Sweetheart," she said, "I don't know how you got the idea into your head that you were going to make felt hats in school."

"Because the teacher said!" I replied. "She *promised.*"

My mother unfolded her hands, clasped them together, folded them again, and then looked at me.

"I wish you would learn to not read more into what people say than what's actually there," she said.

"What does that mean? How can you *read* what people are saying?"

"It means you have to listen carefully so that when people say something, you do not think they mean more than what they actually said, or something different than what they said. Like your teacher saying your were going to make Easter bonnets, and you thinking that you were going to make a regular hat out of felt or straw."

"Mom, it's a paper plate."

"Yes, I know what it is," my mother said. "But...well...aren't you going to try it on so I can see what it looks like?"

I set the violet-blue paper plate on my head, and when I had finished tying the ribbons, my mother quickly put her hand over her mouth.

I knew what that meant. It meant she was trying not to laugh out loud.

"I wish I had never gone to school today," I said.

"Oh, no, it's not that," Mom said. "It's that you, ahhh, you...you remind me of..."

"What?" I asked.

"Well…when I was a little girl, we used to see this lady in town once in a while who wore elaborate hats."

"What kind of hats?" I said.

"Oh, they were different. Big hats. Lots of ribbons. Feathers. Flowers on them sometimes. You really didn't see women wearing hats like that—not for every day around town. And she was one of those women who was kind of bossy to everyone she talked to, whether she knew that person or not. And she always said exactly what she thought. Even if it wasn't very nice."

"Oh," I said.

My mother smiled. "And one time," she went on, "one time when we saw her, it was a terribly windy day. And the wind blew the hat off her head. I don't know why she didn't have it pinned down with hatpins. Or maybe she did. Anyway, the wind blew it out into the street, and a team of horses came along—and ran right over her hat. Smashed it down flat. It looked like a pancake. Sort of like your Easter bonnet is flat, if you know what I mean."

"Oh!" I said. "What happened then?"

"She went out into the street to pick it up. I don't know why. It certainly could not be repaired. Not after those great big horse feet stomped on it and the wagon wheel ran over it."

I thought about the lady with the smashed hat for a few seconds.

"Mom?" I said. "Is it all right if I take this thing off now? The ribbons under my chin are starting to itch."

"By all means, take it off," Mom said.

I untied the ribbons and laid the decorated paper plate on the table.

"You're going to save your Easter bonnet, aren't you?" Mom said.

"Why?"

"Because I'm sure Loretta will want to see it."

So—when I went upstairs to change out of my school clothes—I carried the Easter bonnet upstairs with me and set it on my dresser.

By the end of the week, when Loretta came home on Friday, the purple paper plate was still sitting on the dresser.

"Well," Loretta said when she saw my hat. "Isn't that a pretty color. Sort of reminds me of the violets on the Bluff in the spring."

"That's what Dad said," I said.

"What did Mother say about it?" Loretta asked as she hung up the skirt she had been wearing.

"She said I should not read more into what people say than what's actually there."

"What?" Loretta asked.

"Like the Easter bonnet," I said. "The teacher said we were making Easter bonnets, so I thought we were making real hats."

"Oh, yes, I see," my sister said. "But what I meant was—did she like the color?"

Come to think of it, Mom hadn't said anything about the color.

"I don't know," I said. "She didn't say anything about the color. She just told me about this lady they used see in town when she was a little girl."

"What about it?" Loretta asked as she pulled on a pair of slacks.

"She said the lady was kind of mean and used to wear big hats. And that one time the wind blew her hat off and a team of horses ran over it!"

"Must not have been much left of it after that," my sister commented.

"Mom said it was as flat as a pancake."

"I'll just bet it was flat!" Loretta said as she went to the closet to find a sweater.

"Do I have to wear this thing to church on Easter?" I said, carefully picking up the purple paper plate with two fingers.

"Wear it to church?" Loretta said. "Why do you ask?"

"Because when I said we were going to make Easter bonnets, you said maybe I could wear it to church."

"No, of course you don't have to wear it to church," Loretta said. "Now, let's get supper on the table. Dad and Ingman will be in from the barn soon."

My sister started down the steps, and halfway down, she began to sing—*"Oh, I could write a sonnet about your Easter bonnet and of the girl I'm taking to the Easter Parade..."*

I slowly followed my sister downstairs.

I was never going to get over it that the Easter bonnet I had made in school was nothing more than a paper plate. Although, now that I thought about it, in a way, it *was* like a real hat—even if it was as flat as the hat run over by a team of horses.

About the only good thing was at least I didn't have to wear the Easter bonnet to church on Sunday.

Too bad it wasn't that easy to get out of wearing the light blue skirt and blouse, the white anklets and the black shiny shoes.

[(Irving Berlin's Easter Parade (USA) (1948)]

~ 3 ~
The Easter Bunny

Bright afternoon sunshine streamed through the tall window, and from my place at the kitchen table, I could look up at a patch of blue sky that seemed as smooth and clear as polished glass. Earlier in the afternoon, I had gone outside to see Dusty, but—just like the day when I had flown my kite for the first time—the wind was so cold it made my eyes water. Mom had reminded me that in another month there would be plenty of warmer days, so I had spent most of the afternoon inside. I had helped Loretta clean upstairs. I had read a book for a while. And now I was working on my Sunday school lesson. As I turned to the next page in the book, my father reached under the sink and brought out a stack of egg cartons

"Want go with me?" he asked.

"Are you leaving right now?" I said, setting down my pencil.

Usually I put off doing my Sunday school homework as long as I could, but since I would rather not ride my bike—or my pony—in the cold, biting wind, now was as good a time as any to work on the lesson that had been assigned for tomorrow.

Dad shifted the egg cartons to his other arm. "Yup, we gotta leave right now if we're gonna get back before it's time to feed the cows."

Every couple of weeks, we bought eggs from a farm several miles away, although it was close enough so that the family was considered one of our neighbors. The daughter of the family raised chickens. She also kept ducks and rabbits and calves. But best of all, she owned a horse, a bay gelding named Lucky she had bought when he was six months old. She had trained him herself.

I always hoped when we went to buy eggs I might have a chance to pet Lucky. Sure, I had my own pony, but I never wanted to miss an opportunity that had anything to do with horses.

I stood up and flipped my Sunday school book closed.

"When do you plan on finishing that?" my mother called out from the living room.

"After supper?" I said.

"Promise?"

"I promise," I said. "I've only got a few questions left, anyway."

I went into the porch, put on my denim chore coat, zipped it up, and stuffed my stocking cap into my pocket. If Lucky was in his pasture, I would need the stocking cap.

"Ready, kiddo?" Dad asked. He pushed open the door and stepped outside onto the porch.

"Look," he said, as we walked toward the pickup truck, "the grass is starting to turn green."

Although a few patches of snow remained in the woods, the lawn and most of the fields were bare. I still could hardly believe it, though, when I walked outside and saw the brownish color of the lawn and the fields, rather than the bright white that had been there all winter long.

A short time later we arrived at the neighbor's place. While the daughter went into the house to get our eggs, Dad and I waited in the yard. The trees on the other side of the driveway blocked the cold north wind and it felt almost warm in the sun.

I had been gazing toward Lucky's pasture and wondering if we could stay long enough for me to pet him when Dad spoke up.

"Want a rabbit?" he asked.

I turned toward him. "What?"

"A rabbit," Dad replied. "You know, an Easter bunny."

He pointed to a small piece of plywood with black letters painted on it that said, "Easter Bunnies For Sale. $1."

I had not noticed the sign.

"An Easter bunny? Could I?"

"I don't see why not," Dad replied.

A rabbit! A real, live rabbit! A couple of the kids at school owned rabbits, and I thought they seemed like such nice little animals with their wiggly noses and long, floppy ears.

I happily thought about the idea of my very own bunny rabbit for all of five seconds—until I remembered my mother.

"Dad? If we bring an Easter bunny home, what will Mom say?"

My mother thought that the dog and the cats and the calves and my pony were far more pets than any farm needed

"It's only a little rabbit," Dad answered. "She won't get mad. Besides, when we tell her that it will eat those cabbage leaves she's always complaining are going to waste, she'll think it's a good idea."

Mom did like to let anything go to waste. One of her favorite sayings was 'waste not, want not.' But when Dad suggested that she could save the cabbage leaves for soup, she said she did not like cabbage in soup because it gave her heartburn.

The girl came back with our eggs a few minutes later, and Dad told her that I wanted an Easter bunny. She took us to a little shed near the barn. Inside were dozens of rabbits. Some were in cages on shelves and some were in pens on the floor. One pen had young rabbits. They were not tiny babies, but they were not as big as the other rabbits. Some were solid black and some were brown, and some were black and white and reminded me of Holstein cows.

And then I noticed one little white rabbit sitting in the corner all by himself.

"See any you like?" Dad asked.

"The white one," I replied, pointing.

The girl reached down and grabbed the rabbit by the scruff of his neck. "This one's an albino," she said. "That's why his eyes are pink."

She held out the rabbit and set him into my waiting hands. The young rabbit sat quietly, and when I cradled him to me, he snuggled down in the crook of my arm. His fur was the softest thing I had ever touched, softer even than Dusty's velvety nose or the fluffy fur of a kitten.

Dad stroked the bunny's head with two calloused fingers. "You're a nice little feller, aren't you."

"Should I find a box to put him in?" the girl asked.

"Is this the one you want?" Dad inquired.

"Yes, Daddy, this is the one I want," I said.

Dad pulled his old cracked and faded brown leather billfold out of his shirt pocket, opened it, thumbed through the bills, selected one and handed it to the girl. She tucked it into her pants pocket.

"I'll go and get a box," she said.

While the girl went to the house, I stood with the rabbit cuddled in my arms. His eyelids drooped and then closed tight.

"Well!" Dad said. "That bunny rabbit must like you. He went to sleep."

I looked down at the rabbit.

"How do you know that means he likes me?" I said.

"If he was scared," Dad said, "he'd be wide awake."

A few minutes later, the girl returned with a shoebox like the ones that Dad's work shoes came in.

"He's pretty small, so he'll be okay in here until you get home," she said. She grabbed the rabbit by the scruff of his neck and plucked him out of my arms. The rabbit's hind feet waved in the air, and when she set him in the box, his toenails scrabbled against the cardboard.

"You woke him up," Dad said. "He was sound asleep."

"He'll settle down once I put the cover on," she said.

The girl fitted the cover over the box and then handed the box to me.

"Are you sure Mom won't get mad?" I asked, as we headed across the driveway toward the pickup truck.

"Naaa," Dad said, "she won't get mad. It's only a little rabbit."

Ten minutes later, however, I was not so sure.

"You got a *what*?" my mother asked, setting aside the potatoes she had peeled for supper.

"A bunny," I said, "you know, for Easter. An Easter bunny."

"And what, if I may ask, are you going to do with a rabbit?" Mom said.

"Keep it for a pet?" Dad suggested.

"Hmmmphhh," my mother snorted. "Another pet. That's just what we need around here."

"Now, Ma," Dad said. "I'll build a cage for him in the barn. He won't be any trouble a'tall. And besides, now you'll have something that'll eat your cabbage leaves. Carrot peelings, too, I guess."

"And who is going to take care of it?" my mother asked. "Roy, you have enough to do without taking care of a rabbit."

"I'll take care of him, Mom," I replied. "Dad said he would show me how."

"Another pet," my mother grumbled. "You'd think the cats and the dog and the pony would be enough."

She shook her head and sighed.

"So—" she said. "What color is this rabbit, anyway."

I knew, then, that it was going to be okay.

"He's white," I said, "with pink eyes and the cutest little pink, wiggly nose. Would you like to see him?"

"I suppose," she answered grudgingly.

We had left the rabbit on the porch. I went to get the box.

"Isn't he cute?" I said, setting the little bundle of fur on her lap.

"He's so soft!" she exclaimed, stroking his head and ears with the tips of her fingers.

I glanced at Dad and saw that he had a funny expression on his face—the one that meant he was trying not to smile.

"Why, you're just a baby, aren't you," Mom said as the rabbit snuggled down in her lap and closed his eyes.

I glanced at Dad again and this time he couldn't hold back the smile.

My mother turned steely blue eyes in his direction. "What are you laughing at?" she asked.

"Nothing, Ma," he replied. "Nothing at all."

"I should hope not," she muttered, petting the rabbit while he dozed with his nose tucked under her arm.

Just then, my sister came up from the basement and opened the door into the living room. "Is one jar of green beans enough? Or should I get another one?" Loretta asked as she walked into the kitchen.

She glanced at my mother, and when she saw the white rabbit sitting on Mom's lap, her eyes widened with surprise.

"Hey! Where'd that come from?" she asked as she set the jar of green beans on the counter.

"He's my Easter bunny," I said. "Isn't he cute?"

"While we were waiting for our eggs, I saw that they had a sign about Easter bunnies for sale," Dad explained.

"He is adorable!" Loretta said, stroking the soft, white fur. The rabbit was still sitting with his nose tucked under Mom's arm.

My mother tilted her head so she could see the kitchen clock. "Little bunny, I hate to wake you up, but I've got to start cooking supper."

She gently prodded the rabbit, and he was awake in an instant.

I started forward, but Dad beat me to it. "I've got him, Ma," he said, picking up the white ball of fur. "You're such a soft little feller, aren't you," he crooned, tucking the rabbit into the crook of his arm. "I'm going to build you a nice, big cage so you have plenty of room to hop around in. And you'll have carrot peelings and cabbage leaves to eat. And oats. We've got lots of whole oats. And cob corn, too."

He set the rabbit in the box out on the porch and then put the cover on the box.

"He can't stay in that shoebox," Dad said, coming back into the kitchen. "Have we got any other cardboard boxes, Ma?"

On the way home, we had decided that until Dad could build a cage, the rabbit would be better off staying in the porch.

Mom frowned. "Hmmm, let's see. Cardboard boxes…"

"I've got one upstairs that you can use," Loretta said. "I've been saving it so I can pack up some of my things from the apartment, but you can have it for the rabbit, if you want."

My sister headed for the steps leading upstairs.

A minute later, she returned with a medium-sized cardboard box.

"Will this do?" she asked.

"That'll work good," Dad said. "He only has to stay in the box until tomorrow. I'll build a cage for him tomorrow afternoon."

True to his word, Dad spent Sunday afternoon building a cage. When he was finished, he mounted it on top of the calf pen wall in the barn. It was a large, sturdy cage, and situated as it was, not far from the barn door, handy for reaching inside to get the water dish or to toss in some cabbage leaves. Or to clean it out. Dad had also made a 'cage cleaner.'

My father had taken one of the triangular knives that had once been on the hay mower but was now too dull to cut hay and had bolted it to a handle, long side down. To clean the cage, all I had to do was reach inside and scrape the droppings and used bedding out the door. Then I could sweep it all into the gutter channel a few feet away.

Now that the cage was ready, I went to the porch and picked up the box with my rabbit in it.

As my father had predicted, the white bunny enjoyed munching on whole oats. He also had eaten the cabbage leaves Mom saved for him while she was making supper. And he liked cob corn, too. I had given him a cob of corn, and he had rolled it around with his nose until it became wedged against the side of his box. When the cob of corn could not move away from him, he nibbled off the kernels, his little jaws working busily in a sideways motion.

"Dad's got your house finished," I said as I went down the porch steps. The white rabbit looked up at me, his head bobbing slightly in time with my footsteps as I followed the path across the yard. He seemed happy enough to crouch in the corner on the old faded blue bath towel that Mom said I could put in the box on top of the straw. When we arrived in the barn, I set the box on the floor, picked the rabbit up and held him in my arms.

"Have you decided what you're gonna call 'im?" Dad asked.

"Thumper," I said. "There's a rabbit named Thumper in that movie, *Bambi*." I had not seen the movie. We never went to movies. But I had heard the other kids at school talking about it.

Dad smiled. "It's as good a name as any, I guess. So Thumper it is."

As I stood there holding Thumper, I noticed that the barn cats, who had gotten up from their naps to watch Dad build the cage, were staring at the young rabbit. When they caught his scent, they lifted their noses and sniffed, their whiskers twitching.

Dad frowned. "We're going to have to watch those kitties."

"Why," I asked, looking down at the cats sitting by my feet.

"Because cats can kill a small rabbit," Dad explained.

I spun around to face my father. "What?"

Dad shook his head. "Now don't get yourself all worked up. Just be sure you always latch the cage door so the cats can't get inside."

"But Daddy," I said.

The cats had always been my friends, and of course I knew they liked to hunt mice, although I had never once considered that they might like to hunt rabbits, too.

"After they get used to him, it'll be okay. Besides, when he's full grown, he'll be too big for them to go after," Dad said.

"Are you sure?" I asked, stroking the rabbit's soft, white fur.

"I'm sure," Dad said. "When he reaches his full size, he'll weigh just as much as the cats."

For the next several days, nearly every time I walked in the barn, I found myself plucking cats off the side of the cage. I would come through the door—and sure enough—there would be a cat clinging to the wire mesh, staring at Thumper.

After a week, the cats finally stopped climbing on the calf pen to stare at my rabbit. And after another week, they stopped paying any attention to Thumper at all.

Our dog, Needles, on the other hand, accepted Thumper right away. Although the cats had at first viewed the young, white rabbit as something they could hunt, when I showed the rabbit to the dog, Needles had sniffed Thumper from nose to tail, and then he had turned and trotted off to find something more interesting to occupy his time.

One evening not long after the cats had stopped staring at Thumper, I took him out of his cage while I was waiting for a bucket of milk to carry to the milkhouse. It wasn't time to feed the calves yet, and there wasn't much else to do while I waited. I had been afraid to take Thumper out of his cage before this when the kitties were staring at him so much, but now that they had stopped paying attention to him, I figured it would be all right. The young white rabbit snuggled down in my arms, pink nose twitching as his eyes slowly drooped closed. I turned and walked back to where my father was milking.

"Hah!" Dad said, coming out into the center aisle. "He's asleep."

At the sound of Dad's voice, Thumper's eyes popped open.

"Well," I said, "I don't think he's *quite* asleep."

"How are ya, little feller?" Dad asked, stroking the top of the white head.

Soon Thumper's eyes drooped closed again.

While I waited for the milker, I walked up and down the barn aisle, petting the rabbit, and in a few minutes, I heard Dad shut off the vacuum line.

"Here you go," he said, switching the cover to the empty milker bucket in the aisle. He carried the milker across the gutter channel, and I watched while Dad put the milker on the cow.

"Okay, Thumper," I said. "You have to go back to your cage."

"No, he doesn't," Dad said, stepping out into the center aisle again.

I turned to look at my father.

"But Daddy," I said, "if I put him on the floor, he might wander up by the cows and get stepped on."

"No, he won't," Dad said.

"How do you know?" I asked.

"Because I'm going to hold him while you're gone."

"You are?" I said.

My father nodded and held out his hands. I carefully put the rabbit into Dad's arms.

"Jeepers but you're soft," he said, stroking the rabbit's ears.

While I filled the milk pail, I heard Dad talking to Thumper, telling him he was a good rabbit and wondering if he would like some molasses from the cow feed. The molasses did not always get mixed into the cow feed at the feed mill, and sometimes, if you looked hard enough, you could find chunks of it the size of a walnut. Dusty liked the molasses from the cow feed, too.

I picked up the bucket of milk and carried it down the barn aisle, and as I opened the door, I could still hear my father talking to the rabbit.

I was halfway to the milkhouse—with the bucket clutched in my right hand and my left arm held out to the side for balance—when a strange thought suddenly occurred to me.

I was not at all sure who had *really* wanted an Easter bunny.

Yes, Dad had seen the sign first. But he had asked me if I wanted a rabbit.

And he had told the girl with rabbits for sale that I wanted a rabbit.

So technically, that meant Thumper was mine. Right?

Except that now I was beginning to wonder.

Especially after I returned to the barn and then for the rest of the evening found myself reminding Dad when it was *my* turn hold him.

Like Nobody Else

The school day was over. A few minutes ago, the place was as busy as an anthill, but now after the buses had left, the halls were quiet. That's what Mom said when the grocery store was crowded, or when people were coming and going at the root beer stand on a hot summer evening when we went for root beer after the milking was done, or when people lined up for the Sunday chicken dinner at the fair in June. She said places like that were was as busy as an anthill.

I knew all about anthills. I had seen some big anthills on the Bluff when I followed the cow paths to find the cows so I could bring them up to the barn for milking. A few of the anthills were almost waist high on me. And as I stood beside them, I could see ants crawling around on the mounds of sand—hundreds and hundreds of ants.

Although it was true that the school was much quieter since the buses had left, a few of the kids who lived in town still dawdled in the hallways. And the teachers were still here. And so was one of my classmates. While I waited near the double doors by the office, she came to stand beside me.

"Are you going shopping, too?" my classmate asked, setting a pile of books and papers on the floor by her feet.

I shook my head. "No. My mom is coming for conferences."

She nodded. "My mom's coming to talk to our teacher tomorrow. Today we're going shopping. I need some new shoes for church."

She turned toward the window by the door, and as she looked outside, her mouth popped open in surprise. "Who is *that?*" she whispered.

Out on the sidewalk, my mother made her way toward building, leaning on her forearm crutches, moving one crutch at a time, and then carefully swinging each leg forward. Every six or eight steps, she stopped and took a better grip on the handle of her purse. Other people could have covered the short distance between the curb and the door in a matter of seconds, but for her it was a journey lasting many long minutes.

"That's my mother," I said.

This was going to be the first time I could show Mom to my classroom. Before this, conferences with my teachers had been later in the afternoon, which meant I was already on the bus headed home when she came to school. But today the meeting with my teacher was early enough so I didn't have to ride the bus. For once, I could show Mom to my classroom and then ride home with my parents when the conference was finished.

My classmate turned toward me. "What *happened* to her?"

"She had polio," I replied.

"Oh…" she said

The girl watched my mother for a few seconds longer. "When will she get better?"

I shook my head. "She won't."

My friend remained quiet as my mother moved each crutch forward before taking another halting step.

"What is polio, anyway?" she asked finally.

One time when I was a very little girl, I had asked my mother the same question, and she had explained that polio was a virus. "I woke up one morning in November, feeling like I had the flu," she'd said. "I never dreamed it could be anything else. Polio was a summer disease. People used to be afraid to let their kids go anywhere in the summer because they didn't want them to catch it."

"They wouldn't let their kids go *anywhere*?" I had asked.

"Well, no, they didn't keep them home all the time. But they wouldn't let them go where there were lots of people. I'd heard they even went so far as to close parks. And sometimes when people lived in big cities, they went to the country for the summer."

"Like a vacation?" I wondered.

My mother shook her head. "Not a vacation. They went because they were afraid. But once the weather got colder in the fall, it didn't seem like polio spread so much, and then people stopped worrying. When I thought about it later, though, we *did* have a warm fall that year."

"Then what happened after you woke up feeling sick?" I had asked.

"I just kept getting worse," she replied. "And I had such a terrible backache. Later in the afternoon, I walked out to the pasture to get the cows, and it was like I could hardly drag myself, I felt so tired and my back hurt so much. The next morning, I couldn't get out of bed. A little while later, the doctor came, and then after that, they took me to the hospital in Madison."

When my mother went to the hospital, she had no way of knowing it would be six months before she could come home. Or that her trip to the back of the farm on a sunny November afternoon would be the very last one that she would take anywhere without the help of her crutches. I didn't think my classmate wanted to hear all of that, however, so I tried to think of a good, short answer to her question.

"What is polio? Well, ummmm...polio is sort of like having the flu," I said. "First you get sick, and you're achy and you have a fever, but then it gets worse because you can't walk."

My classmate turned to look at me, her eyes wide with alarm. "Polio is like the flu? Can we catch it?"

"Oh, no," I said. "We can't catch it from Mom. It happened a long, long time ago. Before I was born. Anyway, that's why we get that polio stuff when we get our other shots."

She turned toward the door again. "Why didn't she get any better if it happened so long ago?"

My mother had been stricken with polio in 1942 when she was twenty-six years old, leaving her partially paralyzed in her right leg and completely paralyzed in her left. I was born sixteen years later.

"Well, she *did* get better," I said. "When she had polio, she was really, really sick. She was in the hospital for six months."

"Six months?" my friend echoed. "But that's...that's... that's twice as long as summer vacation."

I turned to look out the door again. "But then she got better and was able to come home again."

Mom said that when Dad came to get her at the hospital, he had driven a Model A Ford. She had gone to the hospital in November but could not come home until May. While she was gone, she had missed her birthday and Christmas with her family, as well as her wedding anniversary, and the birthdays of my brother and sister who were five and three at the time.

The hospital was 250 miles away from our farm, and Dad had driven a Model A Ford all that way to bring her home. I had only seen pictures of Model A cars. They had narrow tires with wire spokes, running boards, and little round headlights that stood out from the side of the hood. The Model A looked like a long, narrow box on wheels with another box over the top where the driver and passengers sat, and it seemed so old-fashioned, I wondered how long it would take to drive five hundred miles in something like that.

By now my mother had reached the door. I went out to hold it open for her.

"Here," Mom said, "would you carry this for me?"

I reached for her purse, although I could not understand why, even after all these years, she insisted on taking it with her everywhere. "It has my wallet, my lipstick, some tissues and a comb. Every lady carries a purse," she had explained several times. It still didn't make any sense to me. Not when it gave her so much trouble.

While I held one door open, my classmate opened the other one.

"Hi, Mrs. Ralph," she said, smiling shyly.

My mother returned her smile. "Thank you very much. That's a big help. I can't push the door open and move through it at the same time."

I started to say something but then decided to keep quiet. Mom could only go through one door at a time, and since part of the doorframe separated the two doors, she didn't need someone to hold the *other* door open.

The three of us began walking slowly down the hall.

"Does it hurt?" my friend blurted after awhile. "The—the—polio, I mean."

"No," Mom said, moving one crutch and then one leg forward. "It doesn't hurt. I just can't walk very fast, that's all."

"I'm sooooo glad. I mean—I'm glad it doesn't hurt."

My mother smiled at the girl once again.

"Uh-oh," my classmate said, her forehead wrinkling.

"What's wrong?" Mom asked.

"I forgot! My mother is supposed to be picking me up. I'd better go see if she's here yet."

And with that, she turned back toward the office.

As we went inside my classroom, I heard someone else ask, "What's wrong with *her*?"

I cringed, embarrassed because the other kids were talking about my mother. For a school that had looked empty only a little while ago, an awful lot of kids suddenly seemed to be here.

"She had polio," I heard my friend reply.

"Polio? What's that?"

I glanced at my mother, hoping that maybe she hadn't heard.

Mom caught my eye. "It's okay," she said quietly. "They're just curious."

When my teacher rose from behind her desk, I left the room to go out and sit in the car with Dad. In the hall, a boy who was a little older than me trotted to catch up.

"Say —" he said. "Did your mom *really* have polio?"

I nodded.

"I kinda thought maybe that girl was making it up when I heard her tell that other kid," he explained. "We learned all about polio in social studies class. Some people even had to stay in what they called an iron lung because they couldn't breathe. Did that happen to your mom?"

I shook my head. She had never mentioned it.

"But now your mom has to walk really slow? And use crutches?" he continued.

"That's right," I said.

"Well—I hope she gets better," he said.

And then he hurried away.

I didn't bother trying to tell him Mom wouldn't get any better. Even though he had learned 'all about polio,' I figured he must have missed the part about how once people got paralyzed, they stayed paralyzed.

I pushed on the bar across the middle of the metal door to release the latch and went out into the sunshine. Dad had parked the car along the driveway in front of the school. I opened the car door and slid into the front seat.

"Did Ma make it in to see your teacher all right?" he asked.

"Yes," I said.

I looked out the window toward the school.

"Daddy," I said, turning back to look at my father, "the other kids were talking about her and staring at her. They wanted to know what had happened to her."

"Well, I suppose they did," Dad said. "They've probably never seen anyone like that."

"But Daddy, what if Mom's feelings were hurt?"

Dad shook his head. "I think it would take more than that to hurt your ma's feelings," he said.

We sat there for a while, not saying much of anything.

"How long are those conferences supposed to last?" Dad asked a few minutes later.

I thought about it for a bit. "I think they're ten minutes. Or maybe it's fifteen."

Dad reached into his pocket for his pocket watch. "It's been that long now. Maybe you should go in and see if Ma needs any help."

I opened the car door and went back into the school. When I turned the corner by the office, I saw my mother coming down the hallway. The boy who had learned about polio in social studies class was walking beside her, carrying her purse.

"I can carry Mom's purse if you want me to," I said, holding out my hand.

"Thank you," Mom said to the boy as he gave the purse to me. "You have no idea how much help that was."

The three of us walked down the hallway, me on one side of my mother and the boy on the other.

"Did you have to be in an iron lung?" the boy asked suddenly.

My mother shook her head. "No," she said. "I didn't."

"Did you have to do—what's it called—phys...physical..."

"Therapy," my mother supplied.

"Yeah, that's it. Physical therapy."

"Yes," Mom said. "I had to do a lot of physical therapy. And I had to have hot wool packs wrapped around my legs."

With me still on one side and the boy on the other, we turned the corner by the office.

"I can hold the door," the boy said, trotting on ahead.

"Thank you," Mom said.

The boy opened the door, and as soon as we reached the sidewalk and the boy had closed the door again, my mother stopped.

"Shoot," she said. "Your teacher gave me a slip of paper about your field trip at the end of the year, but I think I left it on her desk. Would you run back and get it? Here, I can take my purse."

I made sure Mom had a firm grip on her purse, then I went back into the school.

The boy who had held the door open was standing by the office.

"Did your mom forget something?" he asked.

"A slip of paper about our field trip," I said.

I hurried to my classroom, got the piece of paper from my teacher, and hurried back down the hall again, where the boy still stood by the office. Since I rode the bus home every day, I did not know if the boy always hung around school after the buses left, or if he was here today for some particular reason.

As I started to walk past him, he spoke up.

"I like your mom," he said. "She's a nice lady!"

I stopped to look at him. What were you supposed to say when somebody said your mom was a nice lady?

"Thanks," I said.

"I'm glad your mom wasn't in an iron lung," he said.

"Me, too," I said as I headed for the door.

"Does that boy stick around after school every day?" my mother asked when I had caught up with her out on the sidewalk. She looked at me and shook her head. "Oh, never mind. How could I expect you to know? You usually ride the bus home."

When we reached the car, I climbed in the back seat while my mother went about the slow process of getting into the front seat. First, as she stood by the car bent from the waist, she tucked her crutches under the seat so they were out of Dad's way. Then she slowly sat down, half turned, and using both hands picked up her left leg and put it in the car and then her right leg. When she was settled, she pulled the door closed.

Dad started the car. "Is the kiddo doing all right in school?"

"Oh, yes, she's doing fine," Mom replied.

"Who was that boy who opened the door?" Dad asked.

My mother shook her head. "I don't know. But he was awfully talkative. And curious. He sure asked a lot of questions."

"I suppose he's never seen anyone like you before," Dad said.

"I suppose not," Mom replied.

To tell you the truth, I had never seen anyone else like my mother, either. I knew there were other people in the world who were paralyzed, but I had never seen them.

And as we drove home, I thought about what it would be like to have a mother who was just like 'other mothers'—a mother that the kids did not stare at and whisper about and ask 'what happened to her?' A mother who could shake out rugs. A mother who could run to answer the telephone. A mother who could walk down the hill to get the mail.

After a while, I gave up.

Mom wasn't like other mothers. And she was never going to be like other mothers. And no amount of thinking could ever change it.

Besides, if Mom could walk down the hill to get the mail or shake rugs or run to answer the telephone, I wouldn't get to do it.

I didn't care much one way or the other about getting the mail or shaking rugs, but it was an awful lot of fun to answer the telephone.

We did not have a telephone in the house until I started school. Mom said they had taken the telephone out during the Great Depression because they couldn't afford to pay for it, but when I started school, she thought maybe we should have a telephone, in case the school needed to get a hold of her.

The teachers, I'd noticed, were always threatening to call parents for one reason or another, although so far, it had not yet happened to me.

And with any luck at all, it never would.

~ 5 ~
The Village Blacksmith

I had already finished my Saturday chores—shaking the rugs in the porch, sweeping and washing the porch floor and dusting the furniture in the living room. But as I stood outside on the porch steps, I could not decide what I wanted to do. Ride my bike? Ride Dusty? Pick violets on the Bluff? Go and see the kittens in the haymow?

The kittens were too little to pick up and pet, but Dad said if I was quiet, I could peek in the nest and watch them. I had to be quiet because we didn't want the momma kitty to move her kittens. If the momma cat moved her kittens, we might not find them until they were big enough to run around, and then they might grow up wild.

I had sat by the nest a couple of times to watch the kittens, and one day, the momma cat had come to the haymow. She had gone into the nest, groomed her kittens and nursed them, and then while I was sitting there, had picked up one by scruff of the neck, came out of the nest and set it on the bale beside me. The little tabby kitten was big enough to have its eyes open but small enough to be walking around on shaky legs. While the mother cat watched from another bale of hay, I had petted the top of the kitten's head with one finger. After a few minutes, the momma cat picked up the kitten and put it back in the nest.

This was the first time I had actually seen one of the kittens, and I told Dad about the momma kitty and her baby while we were sitting at the supper table that evening. Dad had grinned and said the momma cat must have felt sorry for me sitting there all by myself. My big sister, Loretta, had said that life was full of surprises sometimes.

When I asked about the other surprises, she said that flowers and calves and Easter bunnies could be surprises, too, and that you never knew what surprises might be just around the corner.

As I stood on the porch trying to decide what I wanted to do, I tilted my head back to look at the sky. Then I looked around the lawn, first on the driveway side and then on the clothesline side. The sun was shining out of a bright blue sky, and the grass in the yard had turned a brilliant green after a thunderstorm a few days ago. Dad said the grass turned green after a thunderstorm because lightning put nitrogen into the air. I did not know if that was true. All I knew is that one day the grass was mostly brown, and then after the thunderstorm during the night, the next day, the grass was already starting to look much greener—

Bang! Bang! Bang! Bang!

The sudden noise made me forget about my bike, Dusty, the kittens, and why the grass turns green. What in the world could Dad be doing in the—

Bang! Bang! Bang! Bang!

—machine shed?

I jumped down the porch steps and headed for the shed.

As I walked across the yard, once more came the sound of —

Bang! Bang! Bang! Bang!

I walked beneath the maple tree that grew between the garage and gas barrel. Over the past few days, tiny green leaves had popped out on the ends of the branches, and I knew it would not be long before all of the trees were wearing green leaves. Our dog, Needles, I noticed, was stretched out underneath the tree, nose on his paws, facing the door of the machine shed.

As I reached the shed door, Needles rose to his feet and came to stand beside me, and together, we stood peering into the dark interior. The machine shed did not have any windows, and after the bright sunshine outside, it seemed very dark inside the shed. In a few seconds, my eyes began to adjust to the darkness, and I saw Dad lifting the hammer again. He was kneeling on one knee, elbow balanced on his other leg. On the floor in front of him stood the anvil.

Actually, it was not a real anvil—it was a piece of railroad track. But it worked just as well as an anvil. Whenever Dad needed to shape some metal, he would put it on the piece of railroad track and go to work with one of his hammers.

"What're ya doin' Daddy?"

My father looked up at me. Even though it was still spring, his face was tanned the color of dark brown sugar from hours of driving the tractor to plow the fields for corn and oats.

Dad pointed to the anvil. "I'm trying to see if I can flatten out this piece of pipe on one end so I can make a porch railing," he explained. "I might have better luck with a different hammer, though. Your ma wants me to make a railing so it's easier for her to get down the steps."

He got up and went over to his workbench.

"Hmmmm...let's see. Hammer doesn't need to be too big. But too small won't work," he said.

Dad selected a ball-peen hammer, and whistling under his breath, came back to the anvil. When my father was happy, he would whistle a tune that he made up as he went, a tune that had no beginning or no end but was fun to listen to because I never knew where it was going—up or down or in the middle or sideways or backwards or forwards: *tweet-tweet—tweeeeeet-tweet -tweet — tweet— tweeeeet —tweet-tweet — tweet-tweet — tweet-tweet — tweeeeeet-tweet -tweet*.

All at once, Dad stopped whistling. Holding the ball-peen hammer in one calloused hand that had black grease packed under the nails, he looked at me and drew a deep breath. During the spring, summer and fall, Dad's fingernails were often black with grease.

"Under a spreading chestnut-tree/The village smithy stands/The smith, a mighty man is he/With large and sinewy hands/And the muscles of his brawny arms/ Are strong as iron bands."

I blinked once.

Twice.

Tree? Stands?

He? Hands?

Bands?

Those words rhymed.

And when words rhymed, that meant...

I stared at Dad, unable to believe my ears.

He grinned.

"His hair is crisp, and black, and long/ His face is like the tan/His brow is wet with honest sweat/He earns whate'er he can/And looks the whole world in the face/For he owes not any man."

Dad paused for a moment and frowned, as if he were trying to remember what came next. Then he drew in another breath.

"Week in, week out, from morn till night/ You can hear his bellows blow/ You can hear him swing his heavy sledge (he held up the ball-peen hammer)/ With measured beat and slow/Like a sexton ringing the village bell/ When the evening sun is low."

I did not need to look in a mirror to know that my eyes were as round as the big black coat buttons that Mom kept in her button box. I also knew that I was standing with my mouth open.

Mom said it was bad manners to stand around with your jaw hanging open.

I closed my mouth so abruptly that my teeth clicked together.

Dad was a farmer. Farmers milked cows. They fed calves. They washed milkers. They drove tractors. They cleaned the barn. They planted corn. They cut hay. They raked hay. They baled hay.

Farmers also fixed machinery. And built fences. And calf pens. And took loads of corn and oats to town to have it ground into feed for the cows. Farmers also painted granaries. They harvested oats. They picked corn. They combined soybeans. They helped cows have their babies.

Sometimes farmers even doctored sick kittens and calves.

Farmers did not, however—as far as I knew—recite poetry.

"Dad!" I said. "That's... that's...but that's...that's a POEM!"

My father lifted the chore cap off his head and settled it back where it belonged. "Sure is. And I bet you're wondering where I learned it, aren't you."

I looked at him for a few seconds. "Well, of *course* I'm wondering where you learned it!"

"I learned it in school," he said.

"In *school?*"

Dad was more than fifty years old. Fifty years, we had learned in math class, was a half a century. If Dad had learned the poem in school, it was an awfully long time ago.

"You learned that poem in school? But what made you think of it all of sudden?" I said.

I had been around Dad my whole life, but I had never so much as heard him mention poetry.

My father shrugged and looked at the ball-peen hammer he was holding.

"Doin' this, I guess. With the anvil and the hammer. You know, like a blacksmith—except instead of a chestnut tree, we've got a silver maple."

He pointed to the big silver maple just across the driveway from the shed. The tree, with its large, overhanging branches, was much taller than the garage or the machine shed.

"What's that poem called?" I asked.

"'The Village Blacksmith,'" Dad replied.

"Is there more of it?"

He nodded slowly. "There is. But I don't think I can remember any more."

"Oh," I said.

"To tell you the truth, I'm surprised I remembered that much."

"How come you learned it, anyway?" I asked.

"We all did," Dad said. "We used to learn poems and then recite them for the teacher."

"Really?" I said.

"Don't you have to learn poems in school?" he asked.

I shook my head. "No, we don't have to learn any poems. We learn songs, though. In music class."

"Same thing," Dad said.

"Songs are not poems," I said.

"Sure they are. They've just got music with 'em. That's what our teacher used to tell us."

Dad laid the ball-peen hammer down on the floor and went back to his workbench where he rummaged around until he found a wrench.

As he fitted the wrench onto the end of the pipe so he could hold it better, I thought about what he had said.

"You mean songs are like poems, like Yankee Doodle?—'Yankee Doodle went to town, a-riding on a pony. Stuck a feather in his cap and called it macaroni.'"

Once I had said the words out loud, the song did seem like a poem.

"Yup. Like that," he said. "Well, I guess I'd better get back to work if I'm going to get that railing made today. I don't think you're going to want to stay in the shed. It'll be awfully loud."

He banged the ball-peen on the anvil a couple of times.

Even after Dad stopped banging the ball-peen hammer on the anvil, I could still feel the insides of my ears vibrating. He was right. The sound did hurt my ears. Which is probably why Needles had been napping under the silver maple by the gas barrel rather than napping on the floor in the machine shed by Dad, as he would have done otherwise. Wherever Dad was, you could be sure to find Needles there, too.

"Come on Needles," I said. "Let's go see Dusty."

As the dog and I turned to leave the shed, I heard my father say quietly, "Under a spreading chestnut tree/the village smithy stands..."

On my way out to Dusty's pasture, I decided that if I lived to be a hundred years old, I was never going to get used to the idea.

Imagine that.

Dad reciting a poem.

Finding out that Dad knew a poem by heart was a little like the way I might feel if I found out that Needles knew how to bake a cake—or that Dusty could read—or that one of the barn cats knew how to drive a car.

I guess it was just another one of those things Loretta was talking about when she said that life was full of surprises sometimes.

(The Village Blacksmith; Henry Wadsworth Longfellow—1807-1882)

~ 6 ~
Don't Make 'Em Like That Anymore!

The weather was so warm and sunny that while Loretta was cleaning this morning, she had opened the kitchen window to let some fresh air into the house. The weather had not been warm enough before this to leave any windows open, and a soft breeze carried the whistles of the meadowlarks from the field behind the barn—*tweetle-eeeee…tweetle-eetle-ummm…tweetle-eeeee…tweetle-eetle-ummm.*

I loved to listen to the meadowlarks because meadowlarks meant summer vacation was almost here.

"Would you set the table?" Mom said, interrupting my thoughts about the meadowlarks. "Dad and Ingman will be coming in for dinner pretty soon, and then we can eat."

My mother stood by the stove, stirring a kettle of potato soup. Along with the potato soup, we were going to have cold cut sandwiches. Dad's favorite cold cuts were summer sausage (the kind that came in big, long sticks) and Braunschweiger.

A short while later, after I had set the table with plates and bowls and silverware—and Mom had put the bread and Braunschweiger and summer sausage on plates—Dad and Ingman came into the house. Our dog, Needles came in, too. He sat down by the door, feathery white tail swishing back and forth on the linoleum. As soon as Dad sat down by the table, the dog would sit under the table by his feet, so that he was in between Dad and me.

"Smells good," Dad said as he hung his chore cap on the newel post.

"Sure does," Ingman said.

Dad went into the bathroom to wash his hands and face, and then Ingman washed up, too. Mom, Loretta, and I were already sitting down by the time my father and brother came to the table.

Mom looked over at me and nodded. I folded my hands and bowed my head. "Say it slowly," my mother reminded me.

I had no idea why Mom wanted me to say the table prayer slower. We all knew it by heart.

I drew a deep breath. "By…thy… goodness, all are…fed, we thank…the… Lord for daily…bread….Amen," I said.

"Thank you," Mom said.

"Almost nothin' better than potato soup and sandwiches," Dad said, reaching for the serving bowl of potato soup.

"I don't know why I'm so hungry," Ingman said. "Must be all the nice weather."

"Beautiful day," Dad said, as he filled up his soup bowl. "Couldn't ask for better weather than this."

Mom filled her bowl and then reached for a slice of bread. "If you can spare a little time, I've got a job I want you to do this afternoon."

"What kind of job?" Dad said, slathering a thick layer of butter on his bread.

"Inside or outside?" Ingman asked.

"Inside," Mom said. "It shouldn't take very long."

"Oh, sure, we can spare a little time," Dad said. "I've gotta finish planting that field of corn, but as long as I get out there by two o'clock, I ought to be done by supper."

"Good," Mom said. "I want you to move the piano."

"Is *that* all?" Ingman asked.

"We can do that. Won't take long," Dad said.

Every spring and every fall when my big sister was ready to wash the walls in the living room, Dad and Ingman would move the piano out from the wall so she could clean behind it. One time Loretta and I had tried to move the old upright piano, but we didn't get very far.

My mother shook her head. "No, I don't want you to just move it out from the wall. I want you to move it across to the other side of the living room."

Dad was about to take a bite out of his sandwich but changed his mind. He laid the sandwich on the plate beside his bowl of soup.

"What?" he said.

My brother stopped with a spoon of potato soup halfway to his mouth and looked over at Mom.

"What?" he inquired.

"I said—I want you to move the piano across to the other side of the living room," Mom said.

Dad looked at Mom.

Ingman looked at Mom.

Dad looked at Ingman.

Ingman's eyebrows inched up on his forehead.

"Well," Ingman said, "well…we *were* going to start moving the hay so we can sweep the haymow."

Every year before we began to bale hay in June, Dad and Ingman would work on cleaning out the haymow. They would move the hay that was left and pile it into one corner so they could sweep the floor.

"I thought you said you wanted to finish planting corn," Mom said.

"Ummmm…well…I'll finish planting, and Ingman will start on the mow," Dad said.

"You're going to do no such thing," Mom said. "Not until that piano is moved."

"Why do you want to move the piano?" Ingman asked. "What's wrong with where it is now?"

"I don't want it on that side of the living room anymore," Mom said.

My big sister had not said a word as she ladled out a bowl of soup for herself and made a sandwich. "I'll help," Loretta offered.

Dad turned toward my sister. "No, that's okay. We can do it."

"You can move it right after dinner and still have plenty of time for cleaning the mow and planting corn," Mom said.

"That's what you think," Dad muttered.

My mother turned steely blue eyes in Dad's direction. "What?" she asked in a sharper tone of voice.

"Nothing," Dad said. "Not a thing."

Although I had never once in my entire life said I wanted to learn how to play the piano, we had acquired the old upright a couple of years ago because Mom thought I should take piano lessons. I did not know why she thought I needed piano lessons. No one else in our family played any kind of musical instrument. True, Dad was good at whistling in tune with the radio in the barn. And Loretta had a pretty singing voice. Mom, on the other hand, couldn't carry a tune in a tin bucket—she often said so herself—and I knew she was right because I had sat next to her in church many times.

But—once my mother had made up her mind I was going to take piano lessons—I was going to take piano lessons.

For several weeks, Mom had searched the newspaper advertisements, and at last, she had found a piano. The next evening, Loretta and Mom had gone to look at it, and the deal was settled. When my sister and mother came back home, Mom informed Dad and Ingman that she had bought a piano and that they were going to haul it home Saturday.

The day the piano arrived on our farm was a day much like today: a warm, sunny spring afternoon. I had watched by the picture window in the living room for a long time, and when the pickup truck finally came up the driveway, I had rushed outside.

As I stood on the porch steps, Dad had pulled up by the garage, put the truck in reverse and started backing onto the lawn. The piano, or what I could see of it over the sides of the truck, was covered with a varnish so dark, it was almost black.

Dad backed across the lawn until the truck had reached the steps on the other side of the house. He shut off the ignition, and then he and Ingman opened their doors at the same time and got out of the truck, Dad on the driver's side and Ingman on the passenger's side.

As I walked toward the pickup truck, I couldn't help thinking about the music teacher's small, compact piano. The piano was so small that our music teacher could push it wherever she wanted as she went up and down the hall at school. When we stood around it to sing, everyone could see over the top of it. Pieces of wood hardly any bigger than the legs of a chair supported the keyboard.

Even without standing next to the piano in the back of the truck, I knew I would not be able to see over the top of it. The piano was much too big for that. And instead of pieces of wood not much larger than the legs of a chair, this piano had big round pieces of wood that reminded me of the front porch columns of Southern plantation mansions I had seen pictured in books at school.

I went around to the other side of the pickup truck to talk to my father.

"This is going to take some doing," Dad muttered. He looked back and forth between the piano and the back door leading into the house.

"How come you're bringing it in this door?" I asked.

Our house had two doors. The one we used most often led into the kitchen. The second door opened into the living room—or rather, it opened into a small entryway where you could either go up two steps into the living room, or down a flight of steps into the basement.

Dad glanced at me. "The other door won't work. Not enough room to turn it in the porch. So we wouldn't be able to get it through the kitchen door."

As Dad walked around to the opposite side of the truck, I followed right on his heels.

"Can I help carry it?" I asked.

My father shook his head. "No. I want you to go in the house."

"But why?" I said. "I won't get in the way. I promise."

"This thing is so heavy, if it fell on you, you'd be nothing but a grease spot," Dad said.

I followed Dad around to the other side of the truck. "Why would it fall on me? You're not going to drop it, are you?"

My father shrugged. "Jeepers," he said. "I hope not. We'd never be able to set it up again. It's just that...well...I wouldn't want you to be in the wrong place at the wrong time. Accidents can happen awful quick."

"*Please* go in the house," my brother added.

Up until now, Ingman had been busy measuring the piano and the width of the door. He rolled up the measuring tape.

"We'd feel better if you went into the house," he said.

"But—I want to help!"

"The best way you can help is by going into the house," Ingman said. "I don't know if I've ever tried to move anything quite this heavy. And Dad is right. Accidents do happen fast."

I turned toward the porch. "Oh, all right. I'll go inside," I grumbled.

As I entered the kitchen, my mother turned away from the open west window. "Are they going to bring it in soon?" she inquired.

"I think so," I replied and hoisted myself onto the counter. If I leaned forward and put my nose on the screen, maybe I would be able to watch them unload the piano from here.

"What's taking so long, anyway?" Mom asked.

"They're trying to decide how they're going to get it out of the truck," I said.

Suddenly, we heard a yell that sounded a little like "watch out!"

The yell was followed by a tremendous crash—and then something that sounded like someone had struck all the piano keys at once.

The harsh notes lingered in the spring sunshine for a second or two before dying away into an ominous silence.

Mom and I exchanged glances and then we both leaned toward the window. From here, all we could see was the front of the pickup truck but nothing of the piano.

My mother drew a deep breath. "What happened?" she shouted.

"Oh, nothing," Dad replied in a weary voice. "We just dropped the piano—that's all."

Before Mom could finish saying, "You did what?" I headed for the porch.

"What was *that*?" my sister called out in a muffled voice from upstairs.

Loretta had awakened this morning with a headache. Every once in a while, Loretta got a headache. Mom said they were migraine headaches and that her mother, my Grandma Inga, had suffered from migraine headaches, too. After dinner, Loretta had gone upstairs to lie down for a while.

"Daddy and Ingman dropped the piano!" I yelled over my shoulder.

I hit the screen door with one arm held out in front of me like the football players I had seen on television that Ingman liked to watch.

As soon as I got outside, I saw it.

There was the piano.

Flat on its back.

On the lawn.

It had fallen off the planks Dad and Ingman were using as a ramp.

Dad stood there fiddling with his cap, taking it off and putting it back on his head—which I recognized as a sure sign that he was deep in thought—and my brother was walking around the piano, shaking his head—when Mom pushed open the porch door and came down the steps. The forearm crutches she used to help her walk clicked purposefully as she made her way across the lawn to the truck.

"Did you break it?" she asked.

Dad lifted his cap one last time and set it back on his head.

"Don't think so," he replied.

"What do you mean, you don't think so?" Mom asked. "What are we going to do if it *is* broken? You can fix tractors and balers and corn planters and plows, but you don't know anything about fixing pianos."

The faintest glint came into Dad's eyes. "Guess we'd have to find somebody who *does* know, then, wouldn't we."

My mother sighed. She opened her lips, as if she were going to say something, but then clamped them shut again.

As Mom and I stood there and watched, Dad and Ingman heaved and strained and pushed until the old piano was upright again.

And then we watched as they heaved and strained and pushed and lifted to get it back on the planks.

While Dad and Ingman worked to put the piano back on the planks, my mother kept tossing out helpful remarks—

"Be careful!"

"Don't drop it again!"

"Oh, you're getting it too far over on this side!"

"Now you're getting too far on the other side!"

Finally the piano was back on the planks again.

"Well," Dad said, "that was a lot more work than I wanted to do."

Ingman nodded as he pulled up his t-shirt to wipe the sweat off his forehead. Although it was nice spring day, it didn't seem all that hot. Not to me, anyway.

"Don't bring it in the house yet," Mom instructed as she turned back toward the porch.

Dad pulled a bandanna handkerchief out of his pocket and mopped his forehead. "Why not?"

"I want to make sure you don't scratch the door as you bring it through."

"Scratch the door?" I heard Dad mutter. "We can barely lift this thing. It'll be a miracle if we can get it into the house, never mind not scratching the door."

As luck would have it, Mom was too far away to hear Dad's remark.

I followed my mother into the house, and when we reached the living room, she positioned herself by the door leading to the basement.

"All right," she called. "You can bring it in now."

Because the piano was so big and filled up so much of the door, I could only see my brother.

As my mother and I watched, bit by bit, the piano inched through the door and up the two steps.

After what seemed like a very long time, the bulk of the piano rested just inside the living room. I still couldn't see Dad. But I could hear him.

"Where—" he gasped, "do you—want this thing?"

Mom quickly determined the west wall was the best place for the piano. That way, all Dad and Ingman had to do was turn it around

Twenty minutes later, the piano had reached its final destination.

"I'm glad that's done," Ingman said.

"Me, too," Dad said. "Because now that it's in here, I am not moving it again."

"Well, what do you think?" Mom asked, turning to me. "I'll bet you can hardly wait to start lessons. I know I can hardly wait to hear you play it."

I couldn't ever remember my mother looking quite so pleased with herself.

Now that the piano was finally in the house, it took up most of space along the west wall, and as I stood there next to it, I wondered how I was ever going to learn how to play the thing.

"I hope *somebody* learns how to play it," Dad said, "because I am *not* moving it again."

My mother frowned and turned toward Dad. "That's the second time you've said you are not moving it again. I heard you the first time. I'm not going to ask you to move it."

Ingman grinned. "Do you think this is the time to mention that we dropped it when we were loading it, too?"

"You did WHAT?" Mom asked.

Dad shook his head. "No, no. We didn't drop it when we were loading it." He paused. "Came awful close, though."

My father turned and patted the top of the piano. "Boy," he said. "I bet they don't make 'em like this anymore."

"Probably not," Ingman said.

"Too hard to move, that's for sure," Dad said.

And so, of course, the piano had remained by the west wall in the living room...until today.

My mother did not say anything more about moving the piano while we were eating dinner, but instead waited until Dad and Ingman had finished eating and were both drinking coffee and munching cookies for dessert.

"You know, if you get at moving the piano right away, then we can start cleaning behind it, and then you can get back to planting corn and cleaning the hay mow just that much sooner," Mom said.

"Are you *sure* you want it moved?" Dad asked.

"I'm sure," Mom said.

My father sighed. "I guess we'd better do it now, then."

Loretta pushed back her chair. "I'll have to wash the wall before you move the piano over there," she said, as she started gathering up the dishes.

I helped Loretta clear the table, and when we were finished, she opened the cupboard beneath the sink, pulled out the scrub pail and began filling it with hot water. She poured pine cleaner into the pail of water, and the smell of Christmas trees filled the room—the way Christmas trees smelled when Dad cut into the trunk with a saw when we went to get a Christmas tree every December.

A few minutes later, my sister had finished cleaning where the piano was going to be moved, and then Dad and Ingman went into the living room.

"I'll just stay out here and stay out of the way," Mom said. She turned to me. "You should stay out here, too."

"But can't I watch?" I said.

"Only from the doorway," Mom replied.

My father and brother pulled one end of the old upright out from the wall, and then gradually they turned it until it was pointed out into the room.

"Okay, here we go," said Ingman, who had positioned himself behind the piano. He put his hands against it and began to push while Dad grabbed hold of the front and began to pull. Slowly, the piano started its journey across the room.

When they reached the other side of the living room, they turned the piano again and when it was turned, they carefully, inch by inch, pushed it back against the wall.

"Wheeeeeeew!" Ingman said.

"You can say that again," Dad said.

"You're not ever going to want it someplace else, are you?" Ingman asked.

"Oh, no, of course not," said Mom. "There's really nowhere else to put it."

"I hope not," Dad said.

"Didn't get any easier to move, did it," Ingman said.

"No," Dad said. "It didn't. In fact, I think it weighs more now that it did the day we moved it in here."

"How could the piano weigh more, Daddy?" I asked.

My father shrugged. "I suppose it doesn't. But it sure seems like it."

"Play something," my mother instructed. "Just to make sure they didn't get it out of tune moving it."

"Out of tune?" Dad said, turning to look at Mom.

"Out of tune?" Ingman said.

"Well," Mom said. "You never know."

Dad and Ingman had dropped the piano moving it into the house, but even then it wasn't out of tune. Mom had called a piano tuner who had come the next week. He said it only needed a little tuning, but that otherwise, it was fine.

Loretta helped me carry the piano bench across the room. I opened the cover and pulled out one of the old hymnbooks I kept in the bench. The songs in the lesson books were songs that taught some part of playing the piano so you could get practice at it—but they were not songs you could sing. They were not songs you would ever hear anybody sing.

"What do you want me to play?" I asked.

"I don't care," Mom said. "Pick something."

I flipped through the book until I came to one of my favorites.

"Sing, too," Loretta said.

I put the book on the piano and flexed my fingers the way I had seen Liberace do on television before he started playing. I took piano lessons from a lady who used to be our neighbor. Lillian was kind and patient and was a good teacher. The only problem was—I wasn't a good student, and in spite of hours and hours of practice, I could not play the piano very well. But what I lacked in technique—that's what Lillian called it—technique—I made up for with volume.

"Rock of ages, cleft for me," I sang at the top of my voice as I played the piano to accompany myself. "Let me hiiiide myself in theeee. Let the waaaaater and the blood—"

"Okay, okay, that's enough," Mom shouted.

I abruptly stopped playing.

And here I was just getting to the good part.

"Sounded okay to me," Dad said.

"Me, too," Ingman said.

"I think it's still in tune," Loretta said.

"I wouldn't know," Mom said. "It always sounds the same to me, in tune or out of tune."

"Is it all right if I go out and plant my corn now?" Dad asked.

"Oh, sure, by all means. Go and plant your corn," Mom said.

I folded the hymnbook and stood up to put it back in the piano bench. I still did not really know why Mom thought I should take piano lessons. But I was awfully glad she did.

Even though I wasn't very good at it.

Because without the piano, I would *never* be allowed to make so much noise inside the house.

The Impossible Dream

I could hardly believe it. Here I was, walking along the sandy cowpath in the lane between the Bluff and field, clutching a fistful of birdsfoot violets. Often when I came home from school, my mother asked me to do a job around the house—take clothes off the clothesline outside, go to the basement to get a pan of potatoes for supper, or put away the sheets and pillowcases she had ironed that afternoon.

But today, Mom had asked me to pick some violets.

And since it was such a sunny, warm May afternoon, more like summer, really, rather than spring, I jumped at the chance.

The open spot on the south slope of the big wooded hill behind the barn was so purple with violets I could see them from the school bus when we were still a quarter of a mile away.

In school we had learned that the state flower was the wood violet but that another kind of violet which grew around here was called a birdsfoot violet. Our teacher told us they were called birdsfoot violets because the frilly leaves growing close to the ground looked like a bird's foot. I liked birds. Many birds lived on our farm. Barn swallows and Baltimore orioles and robins and sparrows and sometimes rose-breasted grosbeaks that came to eat the oats scattered on the ground by the granary.

Up ahead in the warm afternoon sunshine, the cows lounged around the barnyard, some standing, some lying down, flicking their ears and tails to chase away the flies. As I reached the barnyard gate, I stopped and switched the violets from one hand to the other. My hand felt sweaty from holding the violets, and I didn't want to ruin them before I got back to the house.

"Mooooo-oooo," said one of the Holstein cows standing in the middle of the barnyard. It was Sweetcorn, the cow who had given birth to her calf on the sidehill in Dusty's pasture one summer and then could not get up afterwards. She had been so sick, she hadn't wanted to eat anything until Dad thought of cutting stalks of sweet corn for her from the garden.

The cows had been back in the pasture earlier today—as they were every day—but they were in the barnyard now because they knew it was almost time to come in the barn for their supper of ground up corn and oats with molasses mixed in to make it taste extra-good.

"Moooooooo," said Sweetcorn again, stretching her nose toward my hand.

"Oh, no—no, no—you can't eat Mom's violets!" I said.

Sweetcorn followed me to the wooden fence by the stock tank.

"Dad will let you in the barn pretty soon," I said.

I climbed over the wooden fence, and when I climbed down off the other side, Sweetcorn stood there watching me.

"Moo," she said.

I heard the crunch of tires on the small stones in the driveway and turned away from the fence in time to see Loretta's car before it disappeared on the other side of the garage. I hurried past the granary, and when I reached the gas barrel, I could see my big sister opening the porch door.

"Hi, Loretta!" I yelled.

I waved the fistful of violets at her, and she waved back and then went into the house.

As I started toward the house again, I looked down. A few of the violets had fallen out of my hand when I waved them at Loretta. I stopped to pick them up, carefully tucking them in with the other violets. Mom said she wanted me to get as many violets as I could carry, so I didn't want to waste any of them. While I was kneeling on the ground, one of the barn cats came to see what I was doing and sniffed at the flowers in my hand.

"Mom wants these so she can make tea," I told the cat.

"Meow," she said as she gazed at me with her green-gold eyes.

When I stood up, the cat trotted in front of me, and as I headed for the porch steps, she laid down in the narrow strip of shade by the light pole where the yard light was mounted. She stretched out her front paws and yawned.

"Is this enough?" I asked, holding up the violets as I walked into the kitchen a minute later.

My mother sat by the table, paging through the newspaper.

"I certainly *hope* it's enough," she said.

For the past few months, my mother had been having trouble sleeping. She either could not fall asleep, or else she would wake up in the middle of the night and could not go back to sleep.

I never had trouble sleeping myself. Almost as soon as I crawled in under the blankets, I was sound asleep, and I didn't wake up until my alarm clock went off in the morning. A couple of weeks ago my mother had read in a magazine that a tea made from wild violets was supposed to help a person sleep, and ever since she had read the article, she had been waiting for the violets on the Bluff to bloom.

"What should I do with them?" I asked.

"Put them in the sink," she said, "so I can rinse them off."

Although Loretta had only arrived home a few minutes ago, she was already coming down from upstairs, dressed in an old pair of pants and an old shirt.

"What are you going to do?" I said as I set the violets in the sink.

"Rake that section lawn of by the lilacs," Loretta said. "I should've done it a long time ago, but it's been so cold and rainy for the past couple of weekends."

She went to the sink and peered down at the flowers.

"Do you really think the violets are going to help?" Loretta asked.

"I have no idea," my mother replied. "But it's worth a try. What harm could come from violets, after all?"

"I suppose so. They *are* only violets," Loretta said. She turned to me. "Do you want to help rake?"

Raking, as far as I was concerned, was the most tiresome chore in the whole wide world—put the rake down on the grass, pull it toward you; put the rake down on the grass, pull it toward you. Over and over and over again.

I looked at my mother, hoping that for once she would come up with something else she wanted me to do.

"Go out and help your sister rake," Mom said.

A sinking feeling settled in the pit of my stomach.

That's what I was afraid she would say.

"No, wait," Mom said. "Before you go out, I want you to help me. I've never washed violets, so I don't know if they're going to fall apart. If they do, it might take two hands to put them on the dishtowel."

Ever since I could remember, I had been watching my mother work in the kitchen with one hand as she held onto the counter with the other to keep her balance.

"Help Mother with the violets, and then you can come out and help me with the raking," Loretta said. "I have a surprise for you."

"A surprise?" I said. "What kind of surprise?"

"If I told you, it wouldn't be a surprise!" Loretta said. And with that, she went outside.

"Do you know what the surprise is?" I said to Mom.

She shook her head and shrugged. "When it comes to your sister, I suppose it could be just about anything."

I watched as my mother put her hands on the seat of the chair, one on each side of her and pushed herself up until she was standing on her feet. Bent from the waist, she grasped the edge of the table with one hand and reached for the stove with the other.

When my mother had gotten a firm grip on the stove, she shuffled her feet until she was close enough to lean down and pull open the drawer.

"Here," she said, holding out a small saucepan. "Would you fill this with water?"

I took the pan to the sink and filled it nearly to the top.

"Good," Mom said. "Now would you please set it on the burner."

I put the pan on the burner. My mother reached to the back of the stove and turned the dial to high.

"By the time we're finished washing the violets, the water ought to be hot enough to make my tea," Mom said.

She reached for the counter next to the stove and, shuffling her feet as she went, made her way along the cupboard until she came to the sink. She turned on the cold-water faucet, leaned on the sink against her forearms and began to rinse the violets.

As I stood by the sink next to my mother, I thought about her idea to make violet tea. One time Mom had said that when she was a little girl and was going to school at the country school a mile from our farm, they used to make May baskets out of strips of paper woven together. If the violets were blooming by the first day of May, they would put violets in the May baskets, along with whatever other spring flowers they could find growing in the woods.

Putting violets into May baskets seemed like a good thing to do with violets.

But how could little purple flowers help anyone sleep?

My mother rinsed the violets under a thin stream of running water, and as she laid them in the empty sink, I picked them up and put them on a clean dishtowel. The violets did not fall apart when they were rinsed, which I didn't think they would because they didn't fall apart when it rained, but still, they were soggy and hardly looked like violets.

"Hmmmmm," Mom said, "now I wonder if I am supposed to use just the flowers? Or the flowers and the stems?"

"What did the article say?" I asked as I folded the dishtowel over the violets.

My mother frowned. "It didn't say anything about *how* to make the tea. It just said, among other things, that wild violets are supposed to help you sleep."

She shrugged. "Well, if the flowers are good, the stems must be good, too. Would you please get a bowl out of the cupboard?"

I opened the cupboard door in front of me, reached for a bowl and set it on the counter while my mother pulled the dishtowel back. She picked up the violets, by twos and threes, and laid them in the bowl.

"Would you please put that over by the stove for me?" she asked.

I set the bowl on the counter by the stove. The water in the little saucepan was already boiling, and my mother inched along the counter until she came to the stove. She turned off the burner and poured some of the boiling water over the violets.

"Now what?" I asked.

"Now I have to let them steep," Mom said.

"Steep? Like a hill is steep?"

"No. It's the same word, spelled the same way, but it means they have to soak in the hot water for a while," she explained. "I'm going to let them sit there until supper, so you might as well go out and help your sister rake."

Oh, yes, the raking.

I had forgotten all about the raking.

After one last look at the violets floating in a steaming bowl of water, I went outside, and with my hand on the railing Dad had made out of a piece of old pipe, slowly walked down the steps. Even though it was a sunny day, the railing felt cold under my hand, and I wondered how cold it would feel during the winter.

As soon as I got around the corner of the house, I saw that Loretta was busy raking leaves into a pile by the lilacs. The silver maples at the edge of the lawn and the lilacs in the middle of the back lawn left plenty of leaves to rake up every spring.

From the tops of the silver maples, Baltimore orioles were singing—*tweet-tweet—tweet-tweet—tweet-tweet-tweeta-tweet.*

I stopped and closed my eyes for a minute to listen. Ever since Dad had pointed out how much birds liked to sing in the springtime, I heard birds singing everywhere.

When I opened my eyes, all at once, I saw something unusual.

"Hey!" I said. "What's that?"

Loretta was raking the lawn with a rake that did not look at all like the rakes we had used before. It had a long handle with something that looked like a big wire fan on the bottom—the kind of fan that you would use to fan your face when it's hot. The other rakes we had used before were made of thick tines like the teeth on Dad's drag, except that the tines on the rake were curved and the teeth on Dad's drag were straight.

"For years we've been struggling to rake the lawn with those old garden rakes," Loretta said. "I decided to buy a couple of rakes that are meant to be used to rake the lawn."

"Garden rakes?" I said. "You mean there's different kinds of rakes?"

"Yes," she said. "Those other old rakes are meant to smooth out the dirt when you plant the garden or after you hoe the garden."

"They are?"

I had never seen any other kind of rake—and did not know there was any other kind of rake.

"I bought two," Loretta said. "The other one is over there."

I turned around, and sure enough, another rake just like the one Loretta was using leaned against the house.

Curious to find out how the rake worked, I took hold of the handle, set the wire fan in the grass and drew it toward me.

When the rake reached my feet, I couldn't help wondering what was wrong with it. I had been helping my sister rake the lawn for quite a few years, so I was pretty sure I knew how to rake—except that *this* rake didn't seem to be working right.

So I tried it again.

And then again.

"Am I doing this the way you're supposed to?" I asked.

Loretta stopped raking and watched me.

"I don't know if there's a wrong way to rake. Unless you turn the rake upside-down," she said.

I pulled the rake toward me one more time.

"But this is so easy!" I said.

The new rake glided through the grass and pulled the leaves from last year along with it in one, smooth pass.

The old rakes caught in the grass and required so much effort to pull them that my arms grew tired after only a few minutes.

Loretta smiled. "Like I said—I don't know why we've been struggling with those old garden rakes for so long."

We only had to finish the lawn around the lilacs and some of the front lawn. In no time at all, with both of us working at it, the raking was done. Before he cleaned the barn tomorrow, Dad would bring the manure spreader behind the house to pick up the piles of leaves and old grass that we had raked up, and then he would spread the piles out in the field.

Loretta and I put the new lawn rakes into the machine shed, and then we went back into the house, where my mother stood by the cupboard, using a slotted spoon to fish the violets out of the bowl.

"They don't look much like violets anymore," I said.

The violets had become a lump of green mush with a few streaks of lavender. I had been wondering if the tea would turn a pretty purple color, but it really didn't look like much of anything.

My sister picked up the bowl and swirled the liquid. "Now what do you have to do with it?" she asked.

"I don't have to do anything more with it—except wait and drink a cup of it before I try to go to sleep," Mom replied.

"What do you think it tastes like?" I asked, staring into the bowl.

My mother shrugged. "As long as it's not bitter, I don't really care."

After we had finished milking in the evening and had fed the calves and had turned the cows outside, I could hardly wait to get back in the house so my mother could tell me what the violet tea tasted like.

"Are you ready to drink your tea yet?" I said as I came into the house.

"No," Mom said, "I'm not ready to drink my tea yet—not until after I've watched the weather."

"The weather?" I said, turning to look at the clock. "But that's a long time from now."

Although I was usually in bed by ten o'clock, under the circumstances, Mom said I could stay up to watch her drink the violet tea.

When the weather forecast was finally over after the ten o'clock news, my mother picked up her crutches and went out to the kitchen. I stood by her elbow and watched as she poured the violet tea into a cup, and then I set the cup on the table for her.

"Aren't you going to warm it up first?" Loretta asked. She, too, had come out to the kitchen when the weather was finished.

Mom shook her head. "I don't think it will make much difference."

She picked up the cup of tea.

"Here goes," she said, taking a sip.

"Well?" I asked.

"Hmmmm," my mother said, shaking her head. "Not only doesn't it look like much of anything, it doesn't taste like much of anything."

"It doesn't taste like *anything*?" I said.

"Not really," Mom replied. "It just sort of tastes a tiny little bit the way grass smells when you cut it."

"That's it?" I said.

"That's it," she said, "and if it doesn't taste like much of anything, I don't suppose it's going to do much of anything, either, although, as long as the cup is full, I guess I might as well drink all of it."

The next morning, I woke up at the usual time, and it was while I was pulling a shirt over my head that I remembered Mom's violet tea. I hurried down the stairs, or hurried as fast as I could without slipping on the narrow steps, and when I came down into the kitchen, my mother was sitting by the table.

"I feel terrible," she groaned.

"What's wrong?" I asked, pulling out one of the kitchen chairs so I could sit down.

"I didn't sleep very well," she said, leaning her head on her hand and running her hand through her hair.

"Why not?" I said.

She looked at me with red-rimmed eyes, as if she had been crying, except I knew she hadn't been crying. This is the way Mom looked when she hadn't slept very well.

"All night long, I dreamed I was being chased," she said.

"Chased by what?" I said.

"I dreamed I was being chased by…well…I feel ridiculous saying this," Mom said, "but I dreamed I was being chased by…well…by pink elephants."

I was pretty sure that I had been listening to every word Mom said, but maybe not—because for just a second there, I was almost positive that my mother said she had dreamed she was being chased by pink elephants.

"They were everywhere," Mom continued. "Big ones and little ones. Life-sized and miniature. In the barn. In the garden. In the house. Under the bed. In the closet. Down in the basement…"

"What kind of pink?" I asked. "Were they pretty?"

Mom stared at me, eyebrows high on her forehead. "Were they pretty? What kind of a question is that?"

"Were they a pretty color of pink? There's all kinds of pink, you know. Dark pink. Light pink. Pink that's almost red. Pink that's a little orange, although I don't like that kind of pink. And sometimes it seems like pink might have a little blue mixed with it."

My mother began to laugh.

"Ha-ha-ha-ha-ha," she chortled. "Hee-hee-hee."

Mom put her head down on her arms. "Ha-ha-ha-ha-ha," she snickered.

My mother lifted her head and looked at me. "Ohhhhh…ha-ha-ha-ha-ha. Tee-hee."

After a few minutes of helpless giggling, she was able to talk again.

"The pink elephants weren't even real," she gasped, wiping the tears out of her eyes. "They were stuffed toys."

"You dreamed about being chased by life-sized stuffed toy pink elephants?" I said.

My mother nodded. "The big ones were out in the barn. The miniature ones were in the closet. The medium-sized ones were in the basement."

"Did I just hear you say that you dreamed about pink elephants?" Loretta asked as she came downstairs.

Mom nodded. "Yes, pink elephants. Lots of pink elephants. All kinds of pink elephants. Pink elephants everywhere."

"Are you going to try the tea again?" I asked. "I can go and pick some more violets for you."

My mother shook her head. "No, no. Once was enough. The article said the violets would help you sleep. But it didn't say anything about strange dreams."

"If that's the side effect, I suppose it's not worth it," Loretta said.

"Not worth it a bit," Mom replied. "I slept all night, but since I feel like I spent the whole night being chased, I would rather lie awake. I think it's more restful."

The pan with the rest of the violet tea was still sitting on the countertop.

"Can I taste the tea?" I asked.

My mother shook her head. "Absolutely not. One person dreaming about pink elephants in this house is enough."

"Mom?" I said. "Why did you dream about *pink* elephants? Why not purple ones, seeing as violets are purple?

"And why elephants?" Loretta said. "Why not cows? Or horses?"

My mother rubbed her eyes. "I wish I knew," she said. "As far as I can tell, there was no rhyme or reason to it."

I turned to look out the kitchen window. From here, in the early morning sunshine, I could see some of the violets on the Bluff.

"Would it be all right if I picked more violets when I get home from school today?" I said. "So we can have them for a bouquet on the table?"

Mom stopped rubbing her eyes. "I would love a bouquet," she said. "Just as long as no one asks me to make tea."

Right away when I came home from school in the afternoon, I went to the Bluff to pick more violets. Usually Mom only allowed one excursion to the Bluff each year to pick violets. She said we had too much work to do to waste time picking flowers. I also knew that in another week, the violets would be gone. Then we wouldn't have any more until next year.

And as I plucked the violets out of the purple sea covering the hillside around me, I found myself thinking of my mother's pink elephants.

Who would have thought that violets could make you dream about pink elephants?

Not Mom, that's for sure.

If she had known, she wouldn't have made the violet tea.

But if she hadn't made the tea, then I wouldn't be out here right now picking more violets. I would be back at the house—putting away the sheets and pillowcases my mother had ironed this afternoon.

And I don't have to say that I would rather be picking violets.

Do I?

~ 8 ~
...Gently Down The Stream

Mom held out an envelope. "Here. Set this by Dad's plate so he will see it when he comes in for breakfast." Before I took the envelope, I turned my hands this way and that, to make sure they weren't so dirty they would smudge the white paper.

Only a few minutes ago, I had been out in the barn carrying milk and cutting the long grass beyond the barnyard fence. Every morning and every evening we cut grass for the calves. Dad said it was good for them to eat some grass. If Dad cut the grass, he used the big scythe. If I cut grass, I used the little hand-held cutter that looked like a miniature scythe. When we gathered up the grass in big armfuls and put it in the manger by the calf pen, the calves acted like it was the best thing they had ever eaten. Dad said that to the calves, fresh grass was like the way we would feel about eating birthday cake with vanilla ice cream.

"What's wrong with your hands?" my mother asked when I had finished inspecting my fingers.

I shook my head as I reached for the envelope. "Nothing. I just want to make sure I don't get it dirty."

Mom shrugged. "I don't think it would matter if you *did* get it dirty. Dad will be more interested in the cash, anyway, I have a feeling."

Even though Father's Day was one whole week away, we were going to give Dad his present now. For a long time my father had been saying he would love to have a fishing boat, and over the past several months the surprise had been almost killing me because—we were getting Dad a boat for Father's Day.

Well...we weren't actually getting him a boat. We were giving him the money so he could buy a boat, although from the amount we had managed to save, it wasn't going to be a very big boat. Nothing at all like the motorboats I saw out on the lake pulling water skiers.

Sometimes when we went over the bridge on our way to town, we could see motorboats on the lake. Dad said he would never be able to own one of those boats, seeing as they cost as much as a tractor. My father liked to stop at implement dealerships 'just to look,' so I knew how much tractors cost, and I knew we didn't have enough in the envelope to buy a tractor.

I never said anything to Mom, but I wondered if Dad was going to be disappointed because he couldn't get a big boat.

Since April my mother had been setting aside a little cash every week, such as a couple of dollar bills she received as change when she went to the grocery store. "If I take out some now and then," she'd said the first time she put money in the envelope "it won't be so obvious."

I had no idea why my mother was worried Dad would figure out we were saving money for his Father's Day present. Mom wrote out the checks to pay the bills and took care of all the bookkeeping herself.

Besides my mother's grocery money and the money Ingman and Loretta put in the envelope, whenever Mom paid me fifty cents for helping her clean the closets or for washing the windows or for scrubbing the basement steps or for cleaning out a cupboard, I would also put money in the envelope for Dad's Father's Day present.

All along, my mother said she wanted to give Dad the money before Father's Day so he could go shopping and would have his boat by the time Father's Day arrived. At first she had thought maybe Loretta or Ingman could buy the boat, but then she wondered where we would hide something that big so Dad wouldn't see it.

I held up the plain white envelope. "Shouldn't we write something on it?" I asked. "Like Happy Father's Day?"

"Oh, shoot," Loretta said.

My big sister was coming down the stairs. She had been sitting in her bathrobe, with curlers in her hair, drinking coffee and talking to Mom when I went out to the barn. While I was outside, she had taken the curlers out of her hair, and now she was dressed in a pair of light pink shorts with a light pink blouse to match.

I only had to look at my sister to know we didn't have church this morning. Our parish had three churches. The big church in the country on the other side of town held services every Sunday. Our little church and the other little church took turns every other Sunday. If we were going to church this morning, my sister would not be dressed in shorts.

"I should have gotten a card for Dad after work on Friday," Loretta said. "But I never gave it a thought."

"Well, since we don't have a card, we can write 'Dad' on the envelope, and then, if you hurry," Mom said, turning to me, "you'll have to time to draw a picture to put inside. You can write 'Happy Father's Day' on the picture."

"That's a good idea," Loretta said.

I looked at Loretta and then at Mom.

A picture?

I was not very good at drawing pictures—not like some of the kids in my class at school. A couple of them could, with a few strokes of a pencil or a crayon, draw a picture that looked just like the thing they were drawing. When I tried to draw something, the more lines I put on it, the worse it got.

"I'm not very good at drawing," I said.

"That doesn't matter," Mom said. "It's the thought that counts."

I turned to look at the kitchen clock. Dad would be coming in for breakfast soon. When I had left the barn, he was in the middle of rinsing the milkers. I knew he would not turn the cows outside until after we had eaten breakfast, but he always scraped the manure from the back of stalls and fluffed the bedding before he came to the house.

Dad had probably already started to fluff the bedding.

I didn't have any time to waste.

My mother tore a sheet out of the notebook where she kept the farm records. It wasn't the kind of paper we used in art class at school, but it was going to have to do.

I went to the catchall drawer and got out my box of crayons. When school was over for the year, I would put the crayons in the drawer, where they stayed until the end of the summer, or until Mom decided they took up too much room—whichever came first. Then I would take them upstairs and dump them into the brown paper bag with the other crayons from other years.

I pulled out a blue crayon and started shading in the bottom half of the paper. The picture would have to have water. And a boat. And people in the boat fishing. And a round sun with long yellow rays on the upper half of the paper.

A little while later, the picture was finished. The people in the boat were only stick figures, but I could barely draw stick figures, so I knew better than to try to make them look like people.

I had no more than finished writing 'Happy Father's Day' in black crayon across the middle of the sky when Loretta spoke up. She had been standing watch by the kitchen window.

"Quick. Dad just came around the garage," she said.

I folded the picture, stuffed it in the envelope, set the envelope by his plate, gathered up the crayons, pushed them back into the box and stashed the box in the catchall drawer.

I turned around in time to see Dad walk into the kitchen.

He stopped short by the door and looked at Mom, Loretta and me. My mother sat at her place by the table, a cup of coffee in front of her. I was still standing by the catchall drawer, and Loretta stood by the sink.

"What's the matter with you?" he asked.

"Why?" I said.

"What would make you ask that?" Mom said.

"Nothing's the matter with us," Loretta said.

"You look like you got caught with your hand in the cookie jar," Dad said.

He gazed at us and then shook his head and shrugged. "So. What's for breakfast?" he asked. "I see you've already got the plates out. I suppose you want eggs or pancakes."

Dad always asked what we were having for breakfast. If Loretta was not at home, he would make eggs or pancakes himself. If Loretta was home, she would make breakfast. It wasn't that my mother could not stand up long enough to make eggs or pancakes—but it was much easier for her if Dad or Loretta made breakfast. And today, it was going to be Mom, Dad, Loretta and me at the table. My big brother was working the seven-to-three shift at the creamery this week.

"How about French toast?" Loretta said.

"Sounds good," Dad said. "We haven't had that in a while."

As he turned toward the bathroom so he could wash up, he glanced at the table. "What's this?" he asked, taking a step closer to look at the envelope tucked under the edge of his plate.

"What's what?" Mom said.

"This," he said, pulling out the envelope.

"Oh, that," Mom said. "It's your Father's Day present."

"I thought Father's Day was next weekend," Dad said.

"It is," Mom said. "Wash up first, then you can open it."

Dad laid the envelope on the table by his plate. He returned a few minutes later smelling of the Ivory soap he had used. While he was in the bathroom washing his hands and face, Loretta had begun to mix milk and eggs and vanilla and cinnamon to make French toast.

My father poured a cup of coffee for himself, sat down by the table and reached for the white envelope with fingers that were as deeply tanned as his face. The tan extended all the way up his forearms and past his elbows to the point where the short sleeves of his blue workshirt rested against his arms.

"Should I open this now?" he asked.

My mother nodded.

I had only tucked the flap inside the envelope, and with one wide thumb, my father flicked open the flap.

"What's this?" Dad asked as he pulled out the sheet of folded paper.

He opened the paper and held it up so he could see it better.

"Nice picture," he said. "A boat and two people fishing." He looked over at me. "I suppose you made this?"

"Yes, Daddy."

"And it says 'Happy Father's Day' on it, too," Dad observed. He looked over at me again. "Thank you very much."

"You'd better look and see what else is in the envelope," Mom said.

Loretta finished putting two slices of French toast into the frying pan. She turned away from the stove so she could watch Dad.

My father reached into the envelope and pulled out a couple of tens and a few twenties. My mother, I noticed, had exchanged the ones and the quarters in the envelope for larger bills.

"What's this for?" Dad asked, holding up the money.

"Your Father's Day present," Loretta said.

"I'm sorry, but you'll have to buy your own present," Mom said.

"My own present?" Dad said.

"Don't you get it, Daddy?" I said, pointing to the picture.

My father frowned. "Get—what?"

Mom drew a deep breath. "The money is for a fishing boat!"

Dad's eyes widened with surprise.

"A what?"

"A fishing boat!" I said.

"A fishing boat?" Dad said, as if he had never heard of such a thing.

"You've always talked about how you'd like to have a fishing boat someday," Mom said.

"We thought maybe you'd better buy it yourself, so you can get the one you want," Loretta explained.

My father loved to go fishing. He did not often have the opportunity during the spring and summer and fall when he was busy with fieldwork, and if we did go, we fished from shore in one of several spots by the river, sometimes for a little while after milking in the evening and sometimes on Sunday afternoon. Although the lake was not far away, there was no good place to fish from shore because either the bank was too steep, or someone had built a cottage. You couldn't very well just walk into a person's backyard and go fishing, Dad said.

As I sat there looking at Dad, all of the possibilities seemed to dawn on him at once.

"A boat!" he exclaimed.

"We were so poor for years and years that we couldn't have even thought about it," Mom said. "But now we can."

"A boat!" Dad said.

"We saved money for a long time," I said.

"Since April," Mom said.

"April!" Dad exclaimed.

"We wanted to buy one and surprise you, but we didn't know what you wanted. And besides, we had no place to hide it," Loretta said.

"A boat!" Dad said.

Loretta turned and flipped over the two pieces of French toast.

"I guess I'm going to have to go shopping tomorrow then, aren't I," Dad said.

"Why can't we go today?" I said.

"It's Sunday," Mom said. "The stores are closed on Sunday."

I had forgotten that it was Sunday.

"Can I come along when you go shopping tomorrow, Daddy?" I asked.

"If you want," he said.

Loretta put two more pieces of French toast on the plate in the oven so the toast would stay warm.

"Do I get to go out for a boat ride, too?" she asked.

"Sure," Dad said. He took out his billfold, tucked the money inside, and then pinned his shirt pocket shut again. Some of Dad's workshirts were so old that the buttons wouldn't stay buttoned, so he used a safety pin to keep the pocket closed. After the billfold had been safely pinned back into his shirt pocket, Dad looked at each of us in turn.

"I've been wishing I had a boat for a lot of years," he said. "And I know just the one I want!"

The next afternoon, when Dad had finished cutting hay after dinner, he was ready to buy his fishing boat.

"What's it going to look like?" I asked as I pulled the pickup truck door shut and settled against the seat.

"Small enough to fit in the back of the truck," Dad said.

"Why does it have to fit in the back of the pickup?" I asked.

"Because then I won't need a trailer for it. We can put it in the truck and go when we want to, after milking or on Sunday afternoons."

None of the boats I had seen on the lake could fit the truck.

Several hours later, just in time to put the cows in and feed them before supper, we returned home.

"I'm going outside to see your boat," Mom said after we had come in the house.

Dad had left the truck parked in the driveway, and we both waited in the kitchen while my mother made her way down the steps.

"Look at that," Mom said as she stood behind the truck and inspected Dad's new boat. "It's so shiny and clean," she said, reaching out to touch the smooth aluminum surface.

"And we got two oars!" I said.

The oars rested in the back of the boat. I leaned forward and picked one up so Mom could see it.

"And," Dad said, opening the pickup door and reaching inside, "we got two life preservers and two floating cushions."

The life preservers were bright orange. One cushion was blue and the other red.

"Are you going to take it out of the truck before you feed the cows?" Mom asked.

Dad shook his head. "No-sir. It's staying right where it is. We're going for a boat ride tonight after milking!" he said.

Later that evening when the milking was finished, Dad and I drove down to the lake in the truck while Mom and Loretta followed in the car. We asked Ingman if we wanted to go, but he said he would rather rest because he had to get up early for work at the creamery tomorrow.

Loretta parked the car so Mom could see the boat landing. The sun had started to drop toward the horizon, but it would be a while yet before dark. Overhead, the sky was a crystal clear blue, and from the trees on the lakeshore came the trilling songs of red-winged blackbirds and the twittering of robins.

"How come we're going out in the boat here, Daddy?" I said.

The boat landing was not very far from our farm, but it was the not the boat landing where we went ice fishing in the winter or where Loretta and I sometimes went swimming on hot Sunday afternoons. This landing was little more than an open spot along the shoreline.

"We're going out here because it's closer to home, for one thing," Dad said. "We really don't have all that much time this evening."

"What's the other thing?" I asked.

"No big speed boats on this part of the lake," Dad said, "so we can take our time getting used to the rowboat."

"Why won't there be any speedboats?" Loretta asked.

"Too shallow. But it's just right for us," Dad said.

Dad, Loretta and I pulled the aluminum boat out of the back of the truck and carried it to the edge of the lake.

"Have fun!" Mom called out from the car. She was sitting with the window rolled all the way down. "Don't forget your life preservers!"

"Nuts," Dad said. "I forgot about the life preservers. I suppose you'd better wear them."

"What about you, Dad?" Loretta asked.

He pointed to a blue cushion sitting on one of the boat seats. "I've got the cushion," he said.

Loretta went back to the pickup truck and retrieved the two orange life preservers. She handed one to me and put the other one on herself.

"You get in first, kiddo," Dad said.

While the back of the little aluminum rowboat bobbed around in the water, I crawled over the seats to the other end and sat down. Then Dad got in. And then Loretta pushed us out a ways farther before hopping in herself. "And awaaaaaay we go," she said.

The evening air was cool and calm, without a breath of wind. Dad picked up one of the oars and used it to push the boat out a bit farther. He fitted first one oar into the oarlock and then the other into the opposite oarlock. He began to row with just one oar, and when he did, the boat turned around. When he rowed with the other oar, the boat turned the other way.

"See how that works, kiddo?" he asked. "When you pull with one oar, the boat goes one way. When you pull with the other oar, it goes the opposite way. The next time we go out, when we've got more daylight, you can learn how to row the boat."

"Can I, Daddy? Really?" I said.

"Yup, really," he said.

Dad straightened the boat out and rowed away from the landing. The marshy smell of the rushes growing along the edge of the lake mingled with the scent of warm air beginning to cool off as the sun dropped toward the horizon. The oars creaked in the oarlocks in time with Dad's rowing—*creak-crock, creak-crock, creak-crock.*

"This is so peaceful," Loretta said.

"Tis, isn't it," Dad replied.

As for me, I could only look around with wide-eyed wonder. I had never been in a boat, and I couldn't decide which I liked more: the way the boat slid through the water or the swirls made by the oars.

All too soon, we headed toward the boat landing, and a few minutes later, we were all back on shore.

"How was it?" Mom asked as we walked toward the car.

"It was heavenly!" Loretta said. "So peaceful."

"I didn't know Daddy could row a boat so good!" I said.

"Of course he can row a boat," Mom said. "He's an expert. He won a rowing contest once."

I could feel my eyebrows creeping up on my forehead.

"You *did*?" I said, turning to stare at Dad.

"And as soon as Dad got into the boat, Aunt Othilia said she knew he was going to win," Mom said.

Aunt Othilia had been my mother's aunt, my grandmother's sister. I did not remember her, although there was a picture of me when I was a baby, sitting on her lap. Aunt Othilia had come from Norway when she was a young woman.

"How did Aunt Othilia know he was going to win?" I asked.

"I wondered the same thing myself," Mom said. "She just kept insisting that by the way he handled the oars, he looked more at home in a boat than any of the others."

My mother smiled. "It took me a while to figure it out," she said. "Aunt Othilia grew up in a seaport in Norway, so I'm sure she saw boats of all kinds."

"And Daddy won!" I said.

"Oh, yes," Mom said. "He was the best of any of them."

"Nothin' I like more than a row boat. You can go where you want to with it, and you can take your time," Dad said. "But this is a better boat than that one was. Much better."

"Why is it better?" I asked.

Dad grinned. "Because it's mine."

I looked at my father for a few seconds before I grinned back at him.

And here I was worried Dad would be disappointed if he couldn't have a big motorboat.

Then again, I never knew he had once won a rowing contest.

And that, of course, made all the difference in the world.

9

Buried Treasure

I tucked my mother's note into my pocket, hopped on my bicycle and rode down the hill toward our next-door neighbor's place. The sun was shining out of a deep blue sky, and all together, it was a fine summer morning. The kind of summer morning, I imagined, that it was in the book I was reading.

In the story, the family had inherited an old run-down farm where they were staying for the summer. The kids in the family thought they were going to be bored, stuck out in the country with nothing to do. But then one sunny summer day, they started finding clues that were supposed to lead them to a buried treasure.

Nothing like that had ever happened to me, and the closest I could come to an adventure today was visiting our neighbor, Hannah Paulson. I did not visit Hannah every day during the summer, but that was only because my mother would not let me. Hannah said I was welcome to come any time. Mom said I should be careful not to wear out my welcome.

When I reached the bottom of the hill, I stood up on the pedals until the bike came to a stop, and then I put one foot on the ground. If it had been up to me, I would have coasted all the way to Hannah and Bill's driveway without stopping, but I knew if my mother ever found out I had done that, she would never again let me ride my bike down the hill.

I could not understand why Mom worried so much about cars. Our place and the Paulson's place were the only two farms on our mile-long stretch of country road, and most of the traffic was either coming to our farm or leaving it: my big brother and sister on their way to work, the milk truck every other day, the school bus during the school year, Dad when we went to town to grind feed, and occasionally, the veterinarian's truck. But Mom said that if I wanted to ride my bike, I had to stop and check for cars.

As I stood with one foot on the ground and the other on my bike pedal, the only sound I heard was the wind in the willow trees growing in the marsh, the gurgle of the small spring beside the driveway and the twitter of birds in the plum bushes next to the spring.

Satisfied that no cars were coming from either direction, I pushed off toward the neighbor's place. Hannah and Bill's farm was directly below our driveway, and the old red barn where there had once been milk cows was directly across the road from the creek running through our pasture. I had been in the old barn a few times. A coat of fresh, bright-red paint covered the outside of the barn, but the roof was full of so many small holes that spots of sunshine dappled the haymow. The round spots of sunlight on the haymow floor reminded me of the light-brown dapples on my pony, Dusty.

I pedaled past the old barn, turned into the driveway and parked my bike next to the white cement block milkhouse. At this time of day, Hannah might be working in her garden at the back of the house, so I went past the hedge planted around the edge of the lawn.

The garden was empty.

I turned and walked through the gap in the hedges and straight up to the back door. A large weeping willow grew in the backyard of Hannah's house, and another weeping willow grew in the front yard near the road. Wild roses and bridal wreath bushes were planted along the foundation of the big, square farmhouse, which was much larger than our house. Mom said our house was only a Norwegian log cabin underneath the white slate siding.

As I lifted my hand to knock, the door swung open.

"I saw you ride your bike down the hill," Hannah explained, holding the door open wider. "Come in! Come in!"

Mrs. Paulson was a retired kindergarten teacher. She and her husband, Bill, had lived in Seattle for a long time. A few years ago, they had bought the farm from a relative of Mrs. Paulson's and had moved to Wisconsin. Bill was the only person I knew who wore a hearing aid, a small square light-brown box he kept in the front pocket of his shirt. A wire dangled down the side of his neck connecting the earplug and the small box.

Hannah, with her wire-rimmed glasses and hair combed in smooth waves swept back from her forehead, liked to wear cotton shirtwaist dresses and a blue-and-white or pink-and-white checkered apron. She suffered from arthritis in her knees and said that the thick-soled shoes on her feet—called 'orthopedic' shoes—helped her knees feel better.

"You're just in time," my neighbor said.

"In time for what?" I asked.

"I'm going upstairs!" Hannah said as she led the way into the kitchen. "A cousin of mine wrote to me looking for some photographs, and I think I know right where to find what she wants. You can come up and help me, if you would be so kind."

I reached into my pocket. "This is from Mom," I said, handing her a note. My mother always sent a note with me when I went to see our neighbor. The notes told Hannah how long I could visit.

Hannah smiled as she took the note from me. My mother and Hannah Paulson talked on the telephone every day. I never knew what they talked about, but Mom would not miss taking a phone call from Hannah for anything in the world.

My neighbor unfolded the note, read it, and then turned to look at the kitchen clock. "You can stay for a little more than hour," she said. "That should give us plenty of time to find the pictures."

Hannah and Bill only used the upstairs rooms for storage. They never had any children, so there were no families with grandchildren to come and stay. The first floor—kitchen, dining room, living room, bedroom, bathroom, and another room at the back of the house with French doors that could also be used as a bedroom—was more than enough room for the two of them. That's what Hannah said, anyway.

Mrs. Paulson opened the door to the stairway. Slowly, carefully, she began to climb while I followed behind her. When we reached the upstairs hallway, she opened one of the bedroom doors.

"Is this like an attic?" I asked as looked into the cluttered room.

"I suppose in a way it is," Hannah said. "It's a bedroom, but I use it the same way I would store things in an attic."

I had never been in a real attic before. Our house didn't have one. But in the story I was reading, the kids had found one of their clues to the buried treasure in the attic of their old farmhouse.

Hannah stood in the middle of the room and slowly turned all the way around. "It's here somewhere," she said. "I know it is."

After another pause, she laughed and pointed to a corner of the room. "There it is! I knew it was here somewhere."

In the corner sat a big black trunk. My neighbor threaded her way between boxes and stacks of old magazines and yellowed newspapers and past a couple of straight-backed chairs covered with a thick layer of dust. A window overlooked the road, and several big, fat, lazy flies buzzed and bumped against the murky panes of glass. The window was closed, and the air in the room felt warm and stuffy.

While Hannah pushed aside one of the old chairs and lifted the lid of the trunk, I turned to look at a stack of magazines on the floor with bright yellow covers. They were *National Geographic* magazines. Bill liked to read *National Geographic* when he wasn't outside tinkering with his tractor or driving out to the field to check on his soybeans.

"Oh, my," Mrs. Paulson murmured. "I had forgotten all about this."

I turned away from the magazines to see what Hannah had found.

Mrs. Paulson was holding a doll wearing a long, black dress, a white lace apron, lace cap, cotton stockings, and black leather shoes.

Although I owned a couple of dolls I had gotten for Christmas over the years, I rarely played with dolls. I would much rather be outside helping Dad or playing with Needles or visiting the kittens in the haymow or riding Dusty. But this doll wasn't like any doll I had ever seen. A tiny pair of thread scissors hung at her waist, along with a tiny purse, and she also wore a choker necklace made of dark-red beads.

"What's she doing in your trunk?" I asked.

"This doll is an antique," Hannah replied. "She has a painted bisque porcelain face. I've always liked her face. She is quite old, and she comes from the Netherlands. The story is that she was buried in a trunk—along with some other valuable items—to keep her safe from the Nazis during World War II."

In school we had learned that 'Netherlands' was another name for Holland. And I knew that the Nazis were the 'bad guys' during World War II. But World War II had happened a long time ago. Before I was born—about fifteen years before I was born, Mom said. So the doll really was old if she had been buried in a trunk during World War II...

Wait a minute. The doll had been *buried*—

"Hey!" I said. "She was buried in a trunk! Like buried treasure!"

"Yes," Hannah said. "Like buried treasure."

Mrs. Paulson held the doll toward me.

"Here," she said. "Do you want to look at her?"

"How come you have her?" I asked as I took the doll. Her face, I noticed, was not smooth like glass, but was slightly rough, the way the oilskin tablecloth on the table at home was slightly rough.

"Oh," Hannah replied as she began to rummage in the trunk again, "the doll once belonged to some relatives of mine." She straightened and turned to look at me. "Would you like to take her home with you?"

I was so surprised I almost dropped the doll.

"Take her home ?" I said.

"Girls and dolls belong together," Hannah said. "Go ahead and take her home with you."

"Oh—but—I—I couldn't. Mom would never let me keep her."

I was certain—without even asking—that my mother would not let me keep the doll. A small bouquet of flowers from Hannah's garden was one thing, but this…

"She will let you keep it," Hannah said. "I will explain that I insisted."

From the expression in her eyes, I knew she wanted me to take the doll home.

What I did not know is why *I* wanted the doll, seeing as I never played with dolls.

Of course, this wasn't actually what I would consider a doll. She was more like a miniature model of a real person. And she *had* been buried in a trunk.

"I promise I will take very good care of her," I said.

Hannah smiled her gentle, kindly smile. "I know you will, dear."

After a while, Mrs. Paulson found the pictures she wanted, and then it was time for me to leave. I carefully set the doll in my bike basket. Hannah stood in the doorway, and when I glanced at her, she smiled and waved. I waved back, and then I turned and hopped on my bike.

When I walked into the house a few minutes later, my mother was talking on the telephone.

"Are you *sure* you want her to have it?" I heard Mom say. "Well…all right…thank you for calling." She hung up the phone and turned around.

"Look what Hannah gave me!" I said.

I held out the doll. Mom took it, fingered the tattered black cotton dress and then looked up at me from her chair by the living room window.

"Her clothes could stand to be washed. And she could use a new dress. Would you like me to make a new dress for her?" she asked.

"Make a new dress?" I said. "But I thought you didn't like to sew."

My mother owned a sewing machine, a Singer that my sister used to make clothes. But I had only seen my mother use it to sew strips of rags together for making rag rugs. I had never watched her make any kind of clothing.

"Well," Mom replied. "That's true. I don't like to sew. But I think I could manage a doll dress."

"Really?"

"Don't look at me like that," Mom said. "Yes, I am perfectly capable of making a dress for the doll."

After dinner, my mother and I went through the ragbag, an old pillowcase where she kept the material she planned to tear into strips and sew together for rag rugs. Mom put a rag rug in front of the kitchen sink. And kept a couple in the porch. And put several in the living room, especially under the rocking chair because she didn't want the rockers to scratch the floor. And there were rag rugs upstairs, too.

The rugs were made out of Dad's old work overalls that were too worn out to patch anymore, old sheets, shirts, and cotton dresses my mother wore during the summer. Once she had torn the material into strips, Mom would sew the strips together, would wind them up into a ball the size of a basketball, and when she had enough to make a batch of rugs, she would ask Dad or Loretta to take the material to a lady who owned a loom.

The ragbag also held odds and ends from my sister's sewing projects.

"What about this?" Mom said, holding up a scrap of black satin material.

"Where did that come from?" I asked.

"It's the lining of my blue wool dress," Mom said. "The one Loretta made for me."

Oh, right. The wool dress. One year at the Sunday school Christmas program when I was a very little girl, I felt like I was catching a cold. I fell asleep with my head on my mother's lap. When I woke up after the program was finished, my cheek was bright red from resting against the scratchy wool. And ever since then, I didn't like the feel of anything made out of wool.

"I think this will make a wonderful dress," Mom said, unfolding the black material and stretching it out in front of her.

My mother rummaged around next to her chair until she found her sewing box. "Let's see, I'll need black thread, for one thing," she said.

Whenever I watched my big sister sew, she always used a pattern.

"Hey!" I said. "I just thought of something. You can't make a dress. You don't have a pattern."

My mother shrugged. "I don't need one. I've got the pattern right here." She pointed to the doll. "I'm going to use her old dress as a pattern to make a new dress."

"How are you going to do that?" I asked.

"I'm going to trace the dress on white paper, cut out the paper, and use it as a pattern to cut out the black material," Mom said. "But instead of a dress, she's going to have a skirt and a blouse."

An hour later, my mother had finished the skirt and was working on the blouse.

"A regular seamstress would say I'm doing a poor job," Mom said as she pushed the needle through the fabric again.

"Why?" I said.

"My stitches are too big," she explained.

I continued to watch as my mother stitched around the top part of the blouse. In no time at all, it seemed, the blouse was finished. Only a little while ago, the black satin material was in the ragbag. But now it was a blouse and a skirt.

"How come you don't like to sew?" I asked.

My mother snipped off the black thread.

"This," she said, "is not sewing."

"It's not?"

She shook her head. "People who like to sew use a sewing machine. And they make clothes for people, not doll clothes out of scraps."

Mom picked up the doll. "Now—I think we ought to wash the rest of her clothes."

The white parts of the doll's clothing were yellowed and ringed with water stains, so for the rest of the afternoon, the white cotton stockings, petticoat, cap and apron soaked in a dishpan of hot water and laundry soap and a splash of bleach. Mom said I shouldn't use too much bleach, otherwise the clothes might fall apart.

After supper I rinsed out the clothes and rolled them up in a towel, and when I came in from the barn, I put them over the edge of the bathtub to dry.

The next morning after I had helped Dad with the chores and we had finished eating breakfast, my mother set up the ironing board. She held onto the ironing board with one hand and carefully sprayed the petticoat and apron with starch with the other hand, and then she ironed them. The only other time I saw Mom use starch was when she ironed the white pants and shirts that Ingman wore to work at the creamery.

When Mom was finished, I went upstairs to get the doll. I put the petticoat on first, then her new black skirt and blouse and then the apron and the cap. Mom threaded a needle and sewed the tiny black purse and the scissors onto the front of her dress, put the leather shoes on her feet and tied the laces.

Instead of tattered and dirty, the doll looked crisp and clean. She smelled clean, too. Sweet. Like flowers. That's what I thought starch smelled like—flowers. Up until now, I hadn't realized how dirty and musty the doll had smelled yesterday.

"Can I take her to show Hannah?" I asked. "I mean, may I?"

My mother turned to look at the kitchen clock. "Yes, you may take the doll. But only stay long enough to show Hannah and then come home again. You were down there a long time yesterday."

Ten minutes later I parked my bike on the Paulson's front lawn and, holding the doll in one hand, knocked on the front door with the other.

"Good morning," Hannah said as she opened the door. "Come in."

"Look!" I said, holding out the doll.

"Oh, my," Hannah said. "Isn't she *beautiful*. Your mother sewed a new dress for her. And you washed the rest of her clothes."

"And she smells good, too!" I said.

Hannah laughed as she reached for the doll and held it up to her nose. "Yes, she does smell good. Like flowers."

No—the doll wasn't the kind of buried treasure that the kids had found in the book, which, I discovered while I was reading before I went to sleep last night, had turned out to be rubies.

I was disappointed that the rubies had not been buried in a treasure chest. The kids had accidentally found them when they were climbing a sandy bank, reached for a bush to pull themselves up, and yanked the bush out of the ground. The rubies were tangled up in the roots.

I still didn't know where the rubies came from or how they were connected to the clues the kids had found. And I wasn't sure I ever would know because there wasn't much of the book left to read.

But as I pushed my bike up the hill a while later, I decided that I wouldn't trade the doll for rubies any day. She was real. She was not like a made-up story in a book. She had been buried in a real trunk. During a real war. By real people. And she was going to sit on my dresser where I could see her every day. When I wasn't busy riding Dusty, that is.

Or playing with Needles.
Or helping Dad with the chores.
Or visiting the kittens in the haymow.

10

Not a Cloud in the Sky

Dad paused in the kitchen doorway. "Come on, Needles, aren't you going outside with me?" he asked. We had finished eating breakfast a few minutes ago, and my father was headed back to the barn to let the cows out, scrape down the barn aisle and to wash the milkers before he went into town to grind feed.

Needles, our cream-colored Cocker Spaniel-Spitz mix, lay underneath the kitchen table where he always stayed while we were eating. He rolled his dark brown eyes in Dad's direction and perked his ears at the sound of his name. But he didn't get up.

"Come on, Needles," my father said once again, patting the leg of his faded blue work overalls.

This time the dog swished his fluffy tail back and forth across the linoleum. But still he didn't get up.

Dad tried calling Needles a couple more times.

"Guess he's not coming with me today," he said as he turned toward the door.

I pushed back the flowered oilskin tablecloth so I could see the dog better. When Dad plowed a field or planted corn or cut hay or combined soybeans—Needles went to the field with him. The dog often would trot up and down the rows behind the tractor. And he could keep at it for hours, although on warm summer days, he would take a break now and then to rest in the shade.

Needles came to the barn, too, while we were milking. After all, he never knew when he might have to break up a cat fight. No matter where Needles was, as soon as the howling and hissing started, he would come on the run, and then he would point his feathered tail and bushy skirts toward the fighting cats and would back up until he came between them. The cats were so distracted by the dog that they forgot what they were fighting about.

Needles also supervised while Dad cleaned the barn. From the time the tractor came out of the shed until it returned from the field pulling an empty manure spreader, the dog followed along.

And when my father got in the pickup truck, Needles was right there to see if he could go for a ride, too.

Needles kept a close eye on everything that went on around the farm, so how come he wanted to stay in the house this morning?

I tried to think of another time when he had refused to go outside with Dad.

But I couldn't.

While Mom and I cleared the breakfast dishes, Needles crept from beneath the table and sat down. He panted and trembled, and his forehead was wrinkled, as if he were worried about something.

"What's wrong with Needles?" I asked.

My mother glanced back at the dog. "I don't know," she replied as she turned on the tap to fill the sink with hot water.

I opened the drawer and pulled out a clean, white flour sack dishtowel. "Do you think he could be sick?" I said.

When Mom looked at the dog again, Needles threw a quick glance in my direction, and then, with his eyes fixed upon my mother, went to the sink. He hesitated only a moment before squeezing himself between my mother and the cupboard door.

"I *was* going to say that I thought he seemed fine," she said, looking down at the dog. "But now I'm not so sure."

Needles peeked around my mother's knees, still panting, trembling and looking worried. His black nose twitched, the tips of his ears quivered, and only the end of his tail moved when I caught his eye.

"Needles, get out from there," Mom said.

The dog looked up at her and then returned to gazing straight ahead.

Because of the polio, as my mother leaned on her elbows while she washed dishes, she sometimes had to shift her weight to keep her balance.

"Needles," Mom said, "you're not making this any easier, you know."

Bit by bit, my mother inched her shoe toward the cupboard. I knew she couldn't see what she was doing because Needles blocked her view of the floor, and any second now, she was going to—

"Mom!—"

"YIPE!"

When the dog yelped my mother flinched.

"Needles!" she said sharply. "Get out of the way!"

But instead of moving, the dog pressed himself more tightly against the cupboard doors. My mother sighed, and from the sound of it, I knew she was getting exasperated.

"Come on, Needles," I said. "You're in Mom's way."

Needles looked up at me. Then he went back to staring straight ahead.

My mother put a handful of washed silverware into the empty sink, and while I rinsed and then dried the knives, forks and spoons, something in the back of my brain seemed to be jumping up and down and waving its arms, trying to get my attention.

It was something to do with Needles.

Something about the way he was acting this morning.

And then it hit me.

"Hey!" I said. "Needles acts nervous like this just before it's going to storm."

My mother paused and looked out the window above the sink.

"Well, yes he does," she replied, "but there's not a cloud in the sky right now."

The kitchen window faced the direction from which storms usually came. I pushed myself on tiptoes to see out the window better. All the way to the horizon, the sky was a clear, cloudless blue. To me, it looked like the most perfect of summer days.

Mom inched her foot forward, and once again, Needles yelped.

"Needles!" she exclaimed. "*Move* if you don't want your toes stepped on!"

Instead of moving, however, the dog pressed even tighter against the cupboard, trying to make himself as small as possible.

My mother sighed. "Well, stay there then," she grumbled. "But don't blame me if I step on your feet."

From the time Needles came to live with us when he was a tiny puppy, my mother had said she did not like dogs, even though when he was little, she had made a warm milk and hamburger mixture for him because she wondered if he needed more protein. As Needles grew from a tiny puppy to a full-grown dog, she allowed him to go in and out of the house only because he was a family pet. My mother complained about the sand he dragged in on his paws, and she hardly ever petted him. For his part, Needles stayed out of Mom's way. He seemed to realize she couldn't get around very well.

But that wasn't the only reason Needles stayed away from Mom. The other reason is that housework made him nervous. The only way my mother could use the vacuum cleaner was by sitting on a chair and cleaning the little section around her—then moving the chair so she could clean the next section—but the vacuum cleaner still bothered Needles. You could see it in his eyes. He would find someplace safe, like under the kitchen table where the floor was covered with linoleum, and would wait there until Mom put the vacuum away.

And when my mother washed the floor, going from section to section on her hands and knees, Needles knew better than to walk across the wet areas and make tracks. She had scolded him once after he'd done that, and since then, if the dog happened to be in the house, he would watch her either from the living room doorway or the small hallway that led to the bathroom or from the porch.

No—Needles did not care for housework one bit. He would much rather be with Dad, supervising the fieldwork or the milking, helping to clean the barn, or riding in the pickup truck.

Except today.

For the rest of the morning, Needles stayed near Mom. When she moved to the bedroom to make the bed, he stood in the doorway and watched. When she went to the living room and sat in her chair by the picture window to work on some embroidery, Needles laid down by the chair. And when she went back into the kitchen to make dinner, Needles laid under the table again where he could see her.

Later on while we washed the dinner dishes, once again, Needles stood between Mom's knees and the kitchen cupboard. I tried several times, but I could not coax Needles into leaving the house. He would shift his eyes in my direction, and then he would go back to gazing at my mother. Once I grabbed hold of his collar, but even though he wasn't a very big dog, his legs were strong from hours of trotting beside the tractor, and I couldn't budge him an inch. After my mother saw that he was so unwilling to move, she told me to let him be.

Later on in the afternoon when Mom took a nap, Needles laid on the floor by the bed. When Mom moved to her chair in the living room to read the mail and to work on her embroidery, once again, Needles laid beside her. And when she went to the kitchen to begin preparing supper, Needles laid under the table where he could watch her.

When my sister came home from work, Needles thumped his tail against the floor. But he didn't get up.

And when Dad came into the house for supper after feeding the cows, Needles rolled his eyes toward the door, swished his tail back and forth and went back to keeping his gaze fixed on Mom.

"Still not himself, is he," Dad commented.

"No," my mother said, "he's not. I could understand it if it was clouding up or thundering because I know he doesn't like storms."

She turned to look at the dog. "But," she said, "as you can see, there's not a cloud in the sky."

"No," Dad said, "there isn't."

"Not even a hint of clouds," Loretta said, pausing to look out the window before she set a plate of bread on the table.

"And I'll tell you something else, too," Mom said. "He's *really* starting to get on my nerves, the way he watches me all the time."

During supper, Needles laid under the table by my mother's feet instead of between Dad and me. And of course, when it was time to go out to the barn for milking, Needles still refused to leave the house.

We had finished milking and Dad was in the milkhouse rinsing the milkers and I was getting ready to go outside to cut grass for the calves when one of the windows on the south side of the barn rattled.

Some of the panes were loose in their frames, and Dad said before winter, he would have to put putty around the windows. So, sure, a few of them were loose, but they didn't rattle by themselves for no reason. The only time they rattled was when a long, rolling boom of thunder came from a storm far away.

I set the grass cutter on the feed box and went outside. To the west, angry-looking blue-black clouds filled the sky above the rows of planted pines at the back of the farm. Overhead, the sky was still clear, but the bank of dark clouds had dropped so low, it was almost as if I could reach out and touch them.

I had never seen clouds like that before. Flickers of lightning darted along the edge of the blackness.

I hurried to the milkhouse.

"Daddy!" I said. "Come and look at the sky."

My father finished rinsing off the milkers and then followed me around to the south side of the barn.

He watched the sky for a minute or two. "Go to the house," he said, "and tell Ma to get in the basement. You and Loretta should go in the basement, too."

Before I could answer, a crack of thunder rolled across the sky in long waves: *ka-booooom-boooooo–oooooo...mmmmmm...booooo... ommmmmmmm.*

This time, the thunder was loud enough to rattle all of the loose barn windows.

When the sound of the thunder had died away, I looked at Dad. "What about you? Aren't you coming in the house, too?"

"Yup," he said. "I'm coming in. Just as soon as I close up the barn. Now go tell Ma to get in the basement."

I galloped toward the house, leaped up the steps, yanked open the porch door and flew into the kitchen.

"Daddy says get to the basement," I said. "Daddy says..."

But there was no one in the kitchen.

"Mom?" I shouted. "Loretta?"

"Down here!" I heard my mother say.

I trotted through the living room to the door leading to the basement steps. Loretta and Needles were waiting at the top of the steps. Mom was halfway down.

"Daddy says get to the basement," I said.

"What about Dad?" Loretta said. "Isn't he coming in, too?"

"He wanted to shut the barn doors first," I said.

If the wind came from the right direction during a thunderstorm, rain would blow into the barn and fill up the gutter channels, so I knew that's why Dad wanted to shut the barn doors.

Several minutes later, my mother reached the bottom of the steps. Loretta went down and handed Mom her crutches. Needles followed Loretta, and I followed Needles.

"I wish Dad would get in here soon," Mom said as we stood huddled together in the middle of the basement. The basement walls were made of sandstone blocks my great-grandfather had quarried from the hill behind the barn. The sandstone never dried out completely, so the basement smelled damp and musty.

The rumble of thunder grew louder, and soon we could see flashes of lightning through the small basement windows.

Needles stood next to Mom, and just like this morning, he was panting and trembling and looking very worried.

A minute later, Dad came down the basement steps. The top of his cap and the shoulders of his blue chambray workshirt were covered with dark blue spots the size of dimes.

"It's raining already, it looks like," Mom said.

Dad nodded. "And it's going to rain harder, too, I have a feeling."

"What's that noise?" I said.

We stood looking at each other, listening.

"Wind," Dad said. "It's getting windy."

Lightning flashed and was immediately followed by a crack of thunder that made the whole house rattle. The rushing, booming sound grew louder.

"I hope we don't lose any trees," Mom said.

"Hope not either," Dad replied.

Then all at once, I heard another sound—*crack-crack—crack-crack-crack—crack-crack.*

"What's that?" I asked.

"Hail," Dad said. "It's hail hitting the roof and bouncing off the side of the house."

"Great," Mom said. "That's just what we need."

"Sure is," Dad said. "It'll shred my corn leaves."

As suddenly as it began, the cracking noises stopped.

No one said anything for many long minutes as we listened to the thunder and the booming of the wind.

After a while, Dad turned and headed for the stairs.

"Where are you going?" Mom asked

"I want to see what it looks like outside," he said.

"Roy, stay here," Mom said. "Don't go up there."

"I'm just gonna take a quick look out the window and I'll be right back," Dad said.

Needles stood up, as if he wanted to follow, but then he turned and sat down by Mom's feet again.

"Are you scared?" Loretta asked.

I swallowed hard. "A little," I said.

"Me, too," Loretta said.

Another sizzling bolt of lightning lit up the basement windows and was immediately followed by a crack of thunder so loud it made my ears hurt.

"That was close," Mom said. "It struck something close by."

"How close?" I said. Dusty was out in her pasture, and I wouldn't want one of the big silver maples to fall on her.

"The Bluff maybe," Mom said.

A minute later, Dad came back downstairs.

"Well?" Mom inquired.

Dad shook his head. "It's raining too hard for me to see much of anything, except that the hail was dime-sized, and I think the tree out front is losing lots of little branches."

"How do you know the hail was dime-sized?" I asked.

"I could see some of it in the grass," Dad said.

Another bolt of lightning lit up the basement windows. I put my head down and clamped my hands over my ears, waiting for the crack of thunder.

I was still waiting for the thunder when Dad spoke up.

"Storm is moving away," he said.

"How do you know?" I said, taking my hands off my ears as the rumble of thunder grumbled overhead.

"Because the longer the time between the thunder and lightning, the farther away the storm is," Dad said.

Gradually the sound of the wind died down, too, and then a while later, we couldn't see any lightning at all although we could still hear the thunder from time to time.

"It's letting up," Dad said at last. "I think we can go upstairs again."

Needles glanced at my mother, and when Dad went upstairs, this time Needles trotted right on his heels.

I followed Needles upstairs, through the living room and into the kitchen.

"It's almost over now," Dad said. He went to the stove, poured a cup of coffee and pulled a handful of cookies out of the cookie canister.

"Might as well have some cookies and coffee while I'm waiting for it to stop raining," he said.

When he had finished his coffee and cookies, Dad got up from the table and went to the kitchen window.

"Hmmph! Look at that," he said.

"What's wrong?" my mother asked. She had sat down by the table as soon as she came upstairs.

I stood beside him and peered out the window. The wind had pushed one of the empty hay wagons down the driveway. While we were milking, the hay wagon had been sitting by the granary. Now it was by the garage.

"The wind pushed the hay wagon," I said.

"And that's the heavy wagon, too," Dad said.

One hay wagon had a heavier frame and had been built out of heavier planks.

"But what I can't figure out," my father continued, "is *how* the wind pushed it."

"What do you mean—how?" Mom asked.

"The wind would have to blow out of the north to push the wagon in this direction," Dad said. "But the wind usually doesn't blow out of the north during a thunderstorm."

Dad went to the north kitchen window. "I see we lost a branch off a maple tree, too," he said.

"We lost a branch?" I said, coming to stand beside him.

Sure enough, the large silver maple by the gate in Dusty's pasture had lost a big branch that was now resting on the lawn.

"If that's the worst that happened—the hay wagon got pushed around and the maple tree lost a branch—we should count ourselves lucky," Loretta said.

"Very lucky," said Mom.

Dad sat down in one of the kitchen chairs and patted his knee. Needles came to stand beside him.

"You knew all along, didn't you," Dad said, looking down into the dog's round brown eyes and stroking his ears.

Needles wagged his tail gently and gazed up into Dad's face.

My mother cleared her throat. "Needles," she said. "Come here."

Needles hesitated, looking first at Dad and then at me before he went to my mother.

"I'm…I'm sorry I was upset with you," she said, patting the top of Needles' head with just the tips of her fingers, as if she were patting a cake in the oven to see if it was done.

I'm sorry I was upset with you?

I could hardly believe my ears.

"You're apologizing to Needles?" I asked.

"Yes. I am. He's been a very good dog today. He was just trying to warn me, and I got mad at him," Mom said.

"Well," Dad said, "I'm not so sure that he was exactly trying to warn you."

"Of course he was," Mom said.

Dad shook his head. "No. I think…well…I think…I wonder…if he wanted to protect you."

Mom turned to look at Dad, dark eyebrows pushed up high on her forehead. "Needles? Trying to protect *me*? Why, of all the silly things. I don't even *like* dogs!"

"Maybe so," Dad said. "But that doesn't mean he doesn't like you."

Needles slowly wagged his fluffy tail while Mom kept stroking the top of his head.

"Yes," she said, "you were a very good dog today."

Needles, I noticed, had the same look on his face as he did the day he had caught a rat in the granary and my big brother had told him he was worth his weight in gold. Too bad Ingman wasn't here to see this. He had left for work at the creamery at two-thirty and wouldn't be home until late tonight.

"But," I said, "how did Needles know *this morning* that it was going to storm *tonight*?"

"It probably had something to do with air pressure and humidity and things like that," Loretta said.

"They say dogs can hear and feel things that people can't," Dad said.

"I've always heard that, too," Mom said. She paused and looked at the dog. "And you know what? The next time you tell us it's going to storm, Needles, I'm going to believe you!"

Twenty minutes later, it stopped raining, and when Dad put on his chore cap so he could go back to the barn to let the cows out, Needles stood up.

"Had enough of being in the house for one day?" Dad asked.

Needles wagged his tail. "Woof!" he said.

I followed Dad and Needles outside. My father and the dog went to the barn, but I went to Dusty's pasture to see if she was all right.

My pony was drenched, but otherwise, she seemed none the worse for the experience.

When I walked into the barn a few minutes later, Needles seemed none the worse for the experience, either. He was panting happily and backing toward two barn cats who were glaring at each other.

Needles had a different job to do now—and he meant to make sure that it got done.

~11~
Crystal Clear

As I helped Dad put feed in for the cows, all I could think of were the rocks I had seen that afternoon. And the bats. Hundreds of bats clinging to the damp walls of the cave. And of the man who had seen a chipmunk run down a hole and who had put a stick in the hole, accidentally let go of it, and then wondered at the strange sound of the stick bouncing off rocks below.

Ever since I had learned about Crystal Cave in school, I had wanted to see it for myself. The cave was only thirty miles from our farm—and it was like the ones pictured in our science book with stalactites and stalagmites. I never knew such a thing existed so close to home, and going down into the cave was like visiting another world. I was glad I had remembered to take a sweater with me. Our teacher had told us it would be cold inside the cave and that even if we went in the summer, we would wish we'd had a sweater if we forgot to bring one. And since it was Sunday, Dad had said—

"Wouldn't you know it," my father said, interrupting my thoughts.

"Wouldn't I know what?" I said.

Dad had opened the barn door to let the cows inside a few minutes ago. He pointed toward at an empty stall where a Holstein heifer was supposed to be.

"You might know," Dad continued, "when we're gone for an afternoon that's when she would decide to have her baby."

And just like that, I forgot about Crystal Cave.

For the very first time ever, Dad had bred a Holstein heifer to an Angus bull. Over the past few years, some of the first-calf heifers had terrible trouble giving birth to their calves. The vet said that if Dad bred the heifers to an Angus bull, the calves would be smaller and then the heifers would have an easier time of it. There was only one thing wrong with the idea. Mom had not wanted to breed any heifers to an Angus bull. She said that half Holstein and half Angus calves wouldn't be worth anything because they couldn't be used as milk cows.

Dad said if the heifers ended up paralyzed trying to give birth to their calves, then we would lose the cow, and losing the cow would be worse than a half Holstein and half Angus calf.

In the end, my mother had reluctantly agreed.

I had only seen Angus cows at the county fair. They were shiny and black and looked at you with soft, friendly eyes. Dad said they were as wide as they were tall. One of them had licked my arm when I reached out to pet it, and Angus cows, I noticed, had rough sandpapery tongues just like Holsteins and Guernseys and Jerseys.

And now the heifer that was going to have an Angus calf had not come in the barn with the rest of the cows. And I knew what that meant. It meant she had gone off by herself to have her baby.

Dad went to the calendar where he kept track of the cows and their due dates. "Thought so," he said. "She's early. By a couple of weeks."

"Who's early by a couple of weeks?" my big brother asked as he walked into the barn.

Dad tilted his head toward the empty Holstein heifer's stall.

"That's the Angus, isn't it?" Ingman said.

Dad nodded.

My brother laid his big, muscular hand on my shoulder. "Why don't you and I look around the Bluff while Dad drives through the pastures. It'll go quicker if we split up."

Looking for newborn calves in the woods and pastures was like a game of hide-'n-seek. Sometimes we found the cow and calf right away, but sometimes it took an hour. Sometimes more.

Today, I hoped we would find them right away because I could hardly wait to see the calf.

"Let's go around the bottom of the Bluff, first," Ingman suggested.

The sun was still high in the sky as we walked across the barnyard. By the barnyard gate, three separate cow paths came together in one large path. The cows could either go down the lane to get to the pasture at the back of the farm or they could go up into the Bluff or they could go into the pasture east of the Bluff.

"If we walk in the pasture next to the fence," Ingman said, "we won't have to fight our way through the blackberries just yet. She won't be in there, anyway. It's too scratchy."

Blackberry canes thicker than my thumb grew around the bottom of the Bluff, and some of the bushes were higher than Ingman's head. Later on, before school started, the blackberries would be ripe, and then Dad and I would go picking blackberries. The briers, I could see, were covered with tiny green berries. A few weeks ago, the blackberries had bloomed, and the scent of the white blossoms had filled the air with a sweetness that smelled good enough to eat.

Unfortunately, underneath the dark green blackberry leaves lurked thorns which could easily tear a hole in my shirt or my pants and leave bleeding scratches on my arms and legs. Dad said it was a wonder anybody ever picked blackberries, seeing as they were so good at defending themselves.

"If we go down to the end of the pasture here, we can crawl through the fence and walk along the north side," Ingman said. "The blackberries won't be so thick on the north side."

The cows had made paths through the blackberry bushes all around the Bluff, but on the north side, where there was more shade, the blackberry canes were not nearly so big.

As we walked along the pasture fence, up ahead, I saw something round and black sticking out of the blackberry briers.

"Look!" I said, pointing toward the spot. "What's that?"

By the time Ingman turned his head, the patch of black had disappeared.

"I don't see a thing," he said.

"It was a black spot," I said. "Or not a spot, exactly, but something black, anyway."

"Maybe it was a bird," Ingman said. "We've got redwing blackbirds across the road where it's wet. Could have been a crow, too. Lots of crows up in the Bluff."

"No," I said. "This wasn't a bird. It was more like—"

I never got a chance to finish my sentence because the black patch suddenly appeared again. And this time, I could also see a forehead...eyes...and ears...

"Look!" I said. "Right there!"

Ingman stared at the blackberry bushes and then grinned. "Son-of-a-gun," he said. "There she is!"

The heifer calmly gazed back at us until something in the thicket of blackberry briers claimed her attention. "M*ooooooo!*" she said.

"Hah!" Ingman said. "Did you hear that? She's talking to the calf. Baby's already been born."

"But," I said, taking a step closer to the fence where just on the other side was a tangle of blackberry bushes so thick that it might as well have been a solid wall, "how are we going to get her out of there?"

My big brother turned to me. *"We* are not going to get her out of there. *I* am going to get her out. I don't want to have to go looking for you, too."

I stood aside as Ingman crawled through the four-strand barbwire fence. He carefully took hold of the closest blackberry cane between his thumb and forefinger, lifted it and turned it away from him. Then he carefully grasped the next cane. And the next one. In a short while, I could not see him at all.

I could hear him, though.

"Yeee-ouch!"

"Jeepers that stings!"

"Wow—that was a bad one!"

"Let go—would you?"

I knew if only the heifer would stay there until my brother could get to her, once he picked up the calf, she would follow along behind him.

"Yooooo-hoooo! Is she still there yet?" I heard my brother call out.

"Yup," I said. "Same place."

"Good!" he said.

The sound of the *ouches, wows* and *jeepers* grew fainter as my brother worked his way farther into the brambles.

Then, without warning, the quiet of late afternoon—broken only by the sound of a light breeze rustling the leaves on the trees and the songs of robins and blackbirds—was shattered by a terrific yell.

"AHHHHH-heeeeee—OUCH! "

The sound of my brother's yell caused the hair to stand up on the back of my neck.

It sounded very much like a yelp of pain.

My stomach took a jump upward and pushed my heart into my throat.

"What's the matter?" I said. "What happened?"

Ingman did not answer right away, and I began to wonder if I should run back to the house to get Loretta. Dad was in the other pasture with the pickup truck, and I knew my mother would not be able to come out to the woods.

"What happened?" I asked again.

"I got stung," Ingman replied.

I still could not see him, although I could tell from the sound of his voice that he had almost reached the heifer.

"You got stung? By a bee?"

"Of course by a bee. What else would sting me?"

I opened my mouth to reply but shut it again just as quickly.

A minute later, Ingman was standing next to the heifer.

"Can you see the baby?" I said.

"Sure can," Ingman said. "And boy—well, hmmmm—what are you, anyway."

Although I could not see what he was doing, I knew he was lifting the calf's tail to determine if it was a boy or a girl.

"And boy," Ingman continued, "is it *ever* a cute little heifer!"

A heifer!

From the time I was a very little girl, I had always wanted to keep every calf born on the place. Dad said we couldn't keep every calf because a herd of bulls running around in the pasture, fighting with each other, wouldn't serve any good purpose, and that if they were steers, that wouldn't help, either, because we needed the pasture for the cows. So I settled for hoping we could keep every heifer calf.

But since this was our first Black Angus, surely we would keep her. Wouldn't we?

"Come on, kiddo," Ingman said. "Up you go."

My big brother disappeared behind the brambles, and when he stood up again, he held a pure black calf in his arms.

"Come on, little lady, let's get you back to the barn," Ingman said as he pushed his way closer to the fence.

The momma cow, I could see, was right on his heels.

I could also see the blackberry briers tearing at his arms and his sleeves and the legs of his blue work overalls.

"Here you go, baby," Ingman said, setting the calf down outside the fence with arms that were crisscrossed with bleeding scratches.

"How's the mother going to get out?" I said.

"She's not," Ingman replied as he climbed through the fence. "We're going to take the baby on this side, and she can come along on the other side."

I looked at the fence from here down to the barnyard. The momma would be able to walk beside her baby the whole way, except that she would be on one side of the fence and her calf would be on the other side.

I wanted to ask my brother where he got stung, but as I looked at his face, I saw that the answer was in plain sight. A big, red welt stood out in the middle of his forehead, and both of his eyes were starting to look puffy.

"Let's get this calf back to the barn before I can't see where I'm going," Ingman said.

With my brother on one side and me on the other, we urged the calf to move forward along the fence. *Moooooooooo!* said the mother. *Maaaaaa!* said the calf, tottering along on legs that were growing stronger and more steady with each step.

"She's really soft," I said, moving my hand lightly along her back. The calf was so shiny she looked wet, but her hair was completely dry.

"And her feet are so cute," I said.

The calf's tiny black hoofs looked as if they had been painted with black fingernail polish.

The other thing about her, of course, is that she was small. Not as tiny as the calves born to our Jersey cow, but she was much smaller than the Holstein calves.

At last we came to the gate leading into the barnyard.

"*Mooooo!*" said the mother.

"*Maaaaa!*" said the calf, rushing forward to stand beside her mamma.

The cow sniffed her baby from head to tail and licked her with a few quick swipes of her tongue. When the cow was finished, the calf moved around to her mother's flank and began to nurse, her small black tail jerking from side to side.

Ingman smiled. "Must have worked up an appetite on her very first walk," he said.

As we stood there waiting for the calf to get done with her snack, I saw the pickup truck coming over the rise in the lane next to the field.

"Dad's coming back," I said, shading my eyes with one hand against the bright afternoon summer sun.

The truck slowly bumped along the rutted lane until Dad pulled up to the gate. He shut off the truck, opened the door and stepped out and then waited while Needles jumped to the ground.

The cow, who had been standing quietly while her baby nursed, took a step forward. As she put her head down and glared at the dog, Needles' cream-colored ears drooped, and the wagging tail came to an abrupt halt. He threw a quick glance over his shoulder to make sure he knew exactly where to find the truck, just in case he should have to make a run for it, and then he backed up a few steps.

If the heifer rushed at Needles and chased him under the truck, it would not be the first time that a cow had come after him.

As the dog moved backward toward the truck, the cow stopped glaring at him and turned her head to sniff her baby.

Dad laughed. "Poor Needles! If knew there was a calf out here, he wouldn't have gotten out of the truck."

My father came closer to get a better look at the calf. "Isn't she a dandy!" he said, running his hand along her back.

He glanced at Ingman and then did a double take. "Say! What happened to you?"

"Got stung," my brother said. "Never even saw what it was. I don't know if it was a honey bee or a wasp or a hornet—or what."

Dad winced and shook his head. "The kiddo and I will get the cow and calf to the barn. You should go to the house. Maybe Ma or Loretta will know what to do for that."

Ingman's left eye was now half swollen shut. "I won't argue with you," he said, turning to walk across the barnyard.

The cow was thirsty after her hard work of giving birth and willingly followed Dad across the barnyard to the water tank. The calf followed her mother. I followed the calf. When the cow had finished drinking, pausing now and then to lift her head before guzzling more of the clear, cold water, she willingly followed Dad into the barn.

We put the cow and calf into one of the empty pens closest to the door, and then Dad got a bucket of feed for. The heifer dug into her supper as if she hadn't seen anything to eat all day, and in the meantime, the baby collapsed in the thick straw, curled her neck around so that her nose was resting on her back feet and closed her eyes.

As we watched the heifer eat, the barn was alive with sound of the cows jingling their stanchions and the twittering of the barn swallows as they flew in and out of the door that opened into the barnyard.

"Momma's hungry and baby's tired," Dad said after a while. "Boy, she sure is a cute little thing, though, isn't she."

"Daddy? We're going to keep her, aren't we?"

Dad lifted his cap, settled it back on his head and shrugged. "She's Angus. She won't give much milk."

"I know," I said. "But—"

"Where's that Angus baby?" called out a voice from the other end of the barn.

It was my big sister.

"Ingman said she's the cutest calf he's seen in a long time, and I just had to come out and see her," Loretta said as she walked down the center aisle of the barn toward us.

"She's taking a nap," Dad said.

Loretta peered through the boards of the pen. "My, but she sure is shiny."

Upon hearing another voice, the calf opened her eyes and lifted her head.

"And what a face. She's got such long eyelashes," Loretta said.

The calf's black eyelashes were longer than any of the eyelashes of the women I had seen in the magazines that my sister subscribed to— *Redbook* and *Ladies Home Journal*, to name two of them.

"Well, I'm not going to make her get up just so I can pet her right now," Loretta said. She turned away from the pen. "Supper's ready, if you are."

"I'm ready," Dad said. "What about you, kiddo."

"Me, too," I said.

When we arrived in the house, Ingman was lying on the davenport with a washcloth tied around some ice cubes on his forehead.

"Does it hurt?" I asked.

He nodded. "Feels like somebody jabbed me with a hot poker. Doesn't feel as bad now, though, as it did a little while ago."

"Is the ice helping?" Loretta asked.

"I think so," Ingman said.

My brother did not feel like eating supper, although by the time we were ready for dessert—strawberry shortcake with whipped cream—he came into the kitchen.

"Let me see your face," Mom said.

Ingman turned toward Mom.

"Looks better than it did, I think," she said. "How does it feel?"

"It aches," he said.

"You should eat some shortcake and then take a couple of aspirin," Loretta said. "Aspirin will get rid of some of the pain."

My brother went around to the back of the table and pulled out his chair. The welt in the middle of his forehead was still red, his right eye was puffy, and his left eye was almost swollen shut.

"Momma and baby okay?" he asked.

"The cow got a drink in the barnyard, and she was eating her feed when we left the barn. Baby was taking a nap," Dad said.

"What are we going to call her?" I asked.

My mother paused in reaching for a biscuit and turned to look at me. "Why do you want to call her anything?" she said. "We're not keeping her, you know. She's Angus."

"Now, Ma," Dad said.

"Seems useless to name her if we're going to ship her next week," my mother said.

I tried to swallow around the lump that had risen in my throat.

Ship her next week?

"Absolutely no sense in keeping her around," Mom said. "She'll just eat food the other calves could be eating."

"Now, Ma," Dad said again.

"Don't you 'now Ma' me," she said. "You know it doesn't make any sense to feed a cow that won't milk very much."

"Well," Dad said, "maybe it *does* make sense."

My mother stopped spooning strawberries over her biscuit and stared at Dad with steely blue eyes.

"If she's bred back to Angus, her babies will be three-quarters Angus," Dad said. "And then we would have a beef calf to sell. The beef calf would be bigger and heavier than the Holstein calves at the same age, I'd be willing to bet. And it would definitely be bigger than the Guernsey calves."

"But Daddy," I said. "She's almost as small as Jersey's calves right now."

We had one Jersey cow in the herd, and that was what we called her—Jersey.

In a heartbeat, I realized what I had said and clapped my hand over my mouth. What was I doing—taking Mom's side of the argument?

Dad grinned. "Oh, sure, she's small right now. But not for long. She'll grow fast and put on weight just as fast."

My mother tapped her finger against her lips. When Mom tapped her finger, I knew she was thinking.

"Well, I suppose maybe we *could* keep just this one. As an experiment. To see what happens," Mom said.

When Dad was sure that Mom was not watching him, his right eye closed in the briefest of winks.

I knew right then that all along, Dad had intended to keep the Angus calf if it was a heifer.

"So—what *are* we going to name her?" I asked.

"Only one thing we *can* call her," Ingman said. "She's pure black—"

Loretta picked up her cup of coffee. "So she needs a name that's just the opposite—"

Dad reached for another biscuit to make a second helping of strawberry shortcake. "And since this is the day we went to Crystal Cave—"

"*Crystal!*" I shouted. "We can call her Crystal!"

My mother winced. "There's no need to yell. We can all hear you just fine."

"Sorry," I said.

Dad spooned whipped cream over the strawberries. "Crystal's a nice name," he said. "We've never had a cow named Crystal."

The next morning, the welt on Ingman's forehead was still red, and his right eye was still puffy and his left eye was still almost swollen shut.

It took nearly two weeks for the welt—and the swelling—to go away completely.

And by the end of two weeks, Crystal had learned to drink from a pail by herself and didn't need to suck the rubber nipple that could be screwed into the side of the pail.

"Jeepers, she's got an appetite," Dad said one evening as Dad, Ingman and I watched her drink a pail of milk mixed with milk replacer.

"She's bigger, too, isn't she," I said.

The tiny black calf was already taller and had started to fill out. And not only that, she was friendly, too. Crystal loved to be petted and brushed. If she had curled up for a nap in the straw, as soon as I came in the pen, she would get right up and come over to me.

"Yup," Ingman said. "She is getting bigger."

"Gonna be almost as wide as she is tall someday, I bet," Dad said.

And you know what?

She was.

And so were the three-quarters Angus calves she gave birth to for many years after that.

~ 12 ~
Sea Monsters and Giant Frogs

My legs were much too long for the swing that hung from the clothesline. Dad had tied the rope shorter so the swing was higher off the ground, and the shorter ropes helped a little, except that now the ropes were so short, the swing could not move back and forth very much.

Dad said someday soon he would make a swing in one of the silver maples that grew along the fence by Dusty's pasture. He even knew which branch he was going to use.

But so far, in between cutting, raking and baling hay and milking cows and going to town to grind feed, my father hadn't had time. If I wanted to swing, I was left with no choice but to use the one hanging on the clothesline.

I sat down in the swing, wrapped my arms around the ropes and tilted my head back. If I couldn't swing, I could at least look at the sky. The summer sun felt hot on my face, and I could hear sparrows chirping by the granary. Not loud, fast chirps, but slow, lazy, quiet chirps, as if they were daydreaming about something else besides the pieces of oats they had found in the grass by the granary door.

I put my feet flat on the ground and pushed until the swing was as far back as it would go. Then I picked my feet up, and—as I watched the blue sky streaked with a few hazy, white clouds—sat still while the swing moved back and forth, back and forth, back and forth.

When the swing came to a stop, I pushed off again.

The sun was so warm, and the back-and-forth of the swing was so soothing, that soon my eyelids began to feel heavy. Maybe it wouldn't be such a bad idea to close my eyes for a little while…

All at once, my eyelids snapped open.

What was that?

I looked toward the machine shed and then the other way, toward the house.

There it was again—

"*Meoooooowwwrrr!*"

"Where are you kitty?" I called.

"Meoooooowwwrrrr!" replied the cat.

The barn kitties used different meows for different reasons: *"Hi, I'm hungry! Please feed me!"* and *"Hi! I'm happy to see you! Please pet me!"* and *"I'm lost! Where are you?"* and *"Go away! I don't like you!"* The cats used the 'go away' meow when two of them were having a difference of opinion. That's what Dad called it—a difference of opinion. The 'go away' meow would bring Needles on the run to break up a cat fight.

But this meow was different from anything I had ever heard before. It sounded scared and forlorn.

"I'm coming kitty cat," I said, stepping away from the swing.

"Meoooooowwwrrrr!" said the cat.

I followed the sound and walked past the little pump house and then past the end of the garage.

Once I reached the other side of the garage, I could tell where the meow was coming from. I trotted across the driveway and looked over the edge of the silo pit.

"Kitty!" I gasped.

In the bottom of the pit, one of our barn cats sat crouched on a floating board.

"Meooooooooooooowwwrrrrrrrrr!" said the cat.

The big round hole in the ground had been next to the barn for as long as I could remember. At one time there had been a silo above it, but all that remained now was an open concrete pit with water in the bottom. As each season passed, more rain and melted snow had filled the bottom of the silo pit. I had no idea how deep the water was, but it was deep enough so that a few old boards floated on the black surface.

The cat was so wet that I couldn't tell which one it was—not until she tilted her head back to look up at me, and I saw the little white patch on the underside of her throat. It was one of last year's kittens, a small brown tabby I called Violet.

After I had brought the kitten into the house to show my mother and had left her alone for a few minutes, she had scampered into the living room and discovered one of Mom's African violets. When I finally found her, she was sitting on the floor, one outstretched paw batting at a leaf she broken off the plant.

I thought Mom was going to be upset about her African violet, but much to my surprise, she told me to get another flower pot from underneath the kitchen sink. She filled the pot with potting soil, stuck the leaf down in the dirt and then watered the pot. "Now I've got another African violet," she'd said.

I leaned forward over the side of the pit so I could see better, and all the while, the cat watched me with her light green eyes.

Last week it had been hot and humid, but this week it was cooler, so at least the water in the pit was not quite as stinky. That was one of the things I did not like about the silo pit. On hot summer days, the silo pit smelled like those puddles in the corner between the barn wall and the milkhouse where the cows liked to stand in the shade—stagnant water and mud mixed with cow manure and urine. The silo pit wasn't that bad. But almost.

The other thing I did not like about the silo pit was the clumps of bubbly-looking green algae. I was pretty sure it was algae, anyway. We had learned about algae in science class at school. Sometimes, too, I wondered if *something else* lived just beneath the surface, a sea monster, maybe, like the Loch Ness monster. One of our books at school had a picture of the Loch Ness monster. Or what someone had claimed was the Loch Ness monster. I figured something that big could not fit in the silo pit. Although, then again, maybe it could...

"Kitty-kitty-kitty," I called out as I leaned against the side of the pit. Instead of smooth concrete, like the barn floor, the silo pit was rough with small stones that reminded me of the candied cherries and red, green and yellow bits of citron rind in Mom's Christmas bread. Dad said the silo pit was rough because the concrete had been mixed with river gravel, but that the barn floor was smooth because the concrete had been mixed with sand.

"*MEE-OWWW!*" exclaimed the young cat. She tried to stand up on the floating board, but when she moved, the board tilted forward.

Violet returned to her crouched position and stared up at me again with her light green eyes.

Violet's eyes were not the only sets of eyes staring up at me. That was the other thing I did not like about the silo pit—the giant frogs. Only a few feet away from the cat a huge green speckled frog sat on a different board. One time I had counted six of the big frogs, sunning themselves on the boards floating in the pit. If they had been small, like the little speckled frogs that lived in the creek below the driveway, it would have been one thing. But these frogs were bigger than my hand. Dad said they were bullfrogs.

For the past few years, Dad had been talking about hiring someone to fill in the silo pit. "If we're not gonna have a silo, there's no sense in keeping the pit," he'd say. "Makes it hard to get around there with the tractor. And besides, it's kind of dangerous having an open pit like that."

But so far, the silo pit remained—rotting boards, frogs, algae, and whatever else might be living underneath the black water.

"How did you get down there?" I asked. "Were you walking around the top, Violet? Or did you jump at a bird flying past?"

Cats would rather not step in little puddles on the driveway, much less jump into something with enough water to float boards.

"Meow!" Violet said. Her expression seemed to say, "Don't just stand there. Do something."

"I wish I knew how you got down there," I said.

As I stood looking at the cat, all at once I realized that *how* she had ended up in the pit was not important. What really mattered is that now she could not get out. Sure, cats were good climbers, but even the best ones could not climb concrete.

I thought for a minute or two.

Would it be possible…?

No. Anybody could see the pit was much too deep to reach the cat from the top.

What about the stepladder?

No, that wouldn't work, either. If I could somehow lower the stepladder into the pit, and if I could also somehow manage to climb into the pit by myself, I would never be able to get out again. The stepladder would not be tall enough to reach the top. Then Violet and I would both need to be rescued. If the sea monsters or the giant frogs or the green clumps of algae didn't get us first.

Of course, the *extension* ladder might be tall enough.

I turned to look at the barn. The extension ladder leaned against the outside wall by the door going into the haymow. Instead of using the built-in ladder nailed to the wall inside the barn, we used the ladder outside during haying season.

I turned back to look at Violet.

Yes, the extension ladder *would* work. I could climb down, get hold of the cat, and then climb back up.

No…that wouldn't work, either.

The tall, two-sectioned ladder was much too big and too heavy for me to carry. I would not be able to get it down from the side of the barn by myself, never mind move it to the silo pit. Bringing the extension ladder would require someone taller and much stronger—

"Don't worry kitty. I'll be right back."

"*Meeeee-ow-rrrrr,*" the cat replied, as if to say, "please hurry."

Dad had not gone to town to grind feed, and he was not out in the field cutting hay because the weather forecast predicted rain tonight, so I knew he was most likely around the buildings somewhere.

I ran to the barn. Both the upper and lower doors had been propped open. But the barn was empty, except for a couple of sleepy cats blinking up at me from the straw.

Where else could Dad be?

I ran out the door and jogged across the driveway to the machine shed. After the bright sunshine outside, the windowless shed seemed dark.

"DAD! Dad? Are you in here?"

"No. I'm over here."

I turned and saw my father standing in the doorway of the granary, holding a broom in one hand.

"What's the matter? What's all the yelling for?" he asked.

I sprinted for the granary. "Daddy! There's a kitty in the silo pit!"

My father set the broom against the doorframe.

"There's a cat?" he asked. "In the silo pit?"

"It's Violet," I said. "And she's floating on a board. And she's really scared. And the only way to get her out is with the extension ladder. Please, Daddy, you've got to bring it. I can't carry it by myself."

Dad nodded, and without a word, headed toward the barn, with me right behind him.

At least I *thought* Dad was headed toward the barn.

When he veered off toward the garage, I almost ran into him.

For a man who claimed that he was not as young as he used to be, Dad was quick on his feet. He sidestepped around me, continued toward the garage, went to a pile of old planks and picked one up.

"What's the board for?" I asked.

"To help the cat," he replied. He turned on his heel and headed toward the silo pit, the plank balanced on his hip.

I hurried to catch up.

"But Daddy," I said. "What about the ladder?"

"We don't need the ladder," he said.

"Then what are you going to do with the board?"

"You'll see."

When Dad reached the pit, he pushed the plank over the edge until one end rested in the water and the other end leaned against the top. Then he maneuvered it around until it was next to the board where the cat was still sitting, wet and miserable.

As Violet saw the plank coming toward her, she carefully rose to her feet. The movement caused her board to tip in the dark water.

"Kitty-kitty-kitty!" Dad called.

"Me-ow," said the cat.

She extended one paw toward the plank but then withdrew and walked back and forth on the floating board.

"Kitty-kitty-kitty," Dad called again in his most coaxing voice. "You can do it. Come on, now. I know you can."

Once more the cat put out her paw and withdrew. Then she carefully sat down on the board and stared at the plank.

"You call her," Dad said.

"Violet," I said. "Violet-kitty. Kitty-kitty-kitty."

Violet looked up at me with her light-green eyes. "Meow!" she said.

"Come on, Violet-kitty. Kitty-kitty-kitty."

Violet crouched. And then, while I watched with disbelieving eyes, she hopped the short distance to the plank. She quickly climbed out of the pit, just like she was climbing a tree.

When Violet reached the top, she jumped to the concrete lip, leaped to the ground and shook herself. Water droplets flew in all directions. She shook herself again, sat down and began to lick her feet dry.

I turned to stare at Dad.

He winked. "Cats are good climbers. And a board's a whole lot easier to carry than the extension ladder."

My father reached down and patted Violet on top of the head. It was the only part of her that wasn't wet.

She paused with one foot held in front of her mouth and looked up at him. "Meee-owww!" she exclaimed.

Dad laughed. "You're welcome."

I bent down to give Violet a pat on the head, too.

"Dad? How did you know Violet was saying thank you?"

He shrugged as he began pulling the plank out of the pit. "What would *you* say if someone helped you get out of a place like that?"

Over the next few days, I was relieved to see that Violet seemed none the worse for her experience, although I also noticed that whenever she came out of the barn, she crossed to the other side of the driveway instead of walking past the silo pit.

A few weeks later, Dad hired someone to demolish the pit. When my father announced that the silo pit was going to be filled in, I began to feel sorry for the bullfrogs. My father said the pit was too deep and that we would never be able to catch them to set them free.

On the day the man came to fill in the silo pit, I watched from the kitchen window as a bulldozer pushed in the sides and then crushed the larger chunks of concrete into pieces to fill in the hole. Mom said it was too dangerous for me to be outside while the bulldozer was working, so I had to be content to watch from inside the house.

After the bull dozer finished, all that remained of the silo pit and its bubbly clumps of green algae, the giant frogs—and whatever else might have been living beneath the black water—was a smooth patch of gravel that had been hauled in to level out the top.

"Should have had that old thing filled in years ago," Dad said one evening while we were on our way to the garden he had planted between the driveway and the pasture fence. To get there, we had to walk right past where the pit used to be.

After the milking was finished in the evening, Dad often liked to visit the garden to see what was blossoming and what was ready to pick and what could be eaten right then and there—peas and green beans and tomatoes and ground cherries and carrots, although we took the carrots to the milkhouse first to wash them. The round, red sun had almost reached the western horizon, and in the clear sky above us, barn swallows flew back and forth, catching mosquitoes.

"Seems kind of funny without the silo pit," Dad said.

I glanced at Violet, who followed along beside us. I wondered why the barn cats liked the garden so much. While we pulled weeds or picked vegetables, the cats would either sit on the lawn and watch, or else they would stretch out in the shade of the corn or the potatoes.

"What's so funny about the pit not being here?" I asked.

"It's odd," Dad replied. "Because I was so used to seeing it. Gonna be a while before I stop expecting the pit to be there when I walk around the corner of the barn."

Dad stopped abruptly. "Oh, nuts," he said.

"What?" I asked.

"I *knew* there was something else I wanted to do—and I keep forgetting," he said.

"What's that?"

"Your new swing," Dad replied.

From here, I could see the swing hanging on the end of the clothesline, but I could not see the tree branch on the other side of the house where Dad was going to put the new swing.

"I bet Violet doesn't care about my new swing," I said.

"Huh?" Dad said.

"If I'd had my new swing, I would have been on the other side of the house when she fell in the silo pit," I said.

Dad looked at the tabby cat sitting underneath the arching leaves of the corn plants with her tail curled around her front paws.

"What does that have to do with it?" he asked.

"If I was in back of the house, I don't think I would've been able to hear her," I said.

"Oh, I suppose you're probably right," Dad said. He paused. "Well, it's like they say, I guess—no time like the present. Should we put up a new swing?"

"Could we?"

He nodded. "I think we've got time before it gets too dark."

"Come here, Violet," I said.

The cat left her spot beneath the corn. When I picked her up, she snuggled down in my arms and began to purr—loud, raspy and rumbling.

Dad smiled. "You're a happy cat, aren't you."

Well, one thing about it, anyway. As we walked over the new patch of gravel by the barn, I knew I would never have to worry that Violet would fall into the silo pit again.

I still couldn't help feeling a *little* sorry for the frogs, though—now that they were gone.

.

****

~ 13 ~
Splitting Hairs

Outside most of the light had drained from the sky, and through the open kitchen window came the sound of a whip-poor-will. The crickets were singing, too. Dad said that the warmer it was outside, the faster the crickets sang. He had pointed that out one evening when the temperature had dropped to fifty degrees, and the crickets had slowed down in the cool night air.

Since then, I had paid attention to how fast the crickets were singing, although right now, the pain in my head seemed more important than the crickets—

"Yeee-OUCH!" I screeched.

I turned around to look at my mother.

"Must you yell so loud?" Mom inquired as she delicately plucked a snarl off the comb and dropped it onto the pile.

"But—it hurts."

"Sit still," Mom said. "If you keep jumping around, it's just going to take that much longer."

"But—OW—oooooo—ouch!"

"If you think I'm bad, you should have had *my* mother comb your hair," Mom said. "I always used to wonder if I'd have anything left on my head by the time she got through."

This was the same old story. Every time Mom combed my hair, she would tell me about Grandma Inga.

Somehow, knowing that Grandma Inga was worse than Mom didn't make me feel any better. For one thing, Grandma Inga had died many years before I was born. And for another thing, Mom said that Grandma Inga wasn't much more than five feet tall and that she only weighed a hundred pounds soaking wet.

It seemed to me that someone who was about as tall as the barn broom and who only weighed as much as a bag of oats could not have been very strong—not strong enough to make my head hurt this much.

"If you wouldn't run around outside in the wind, we wouldn't have this problem," Mom said as the comb tore through another snarl.

"What—OW!—should I do?" I asked. "Stay inside all day?"

Just the thought of staying inside on a warm, sunny, summer day made me feel cooped up and sad and maybe even a little grumpy. I would much rather be outside riding my pony, Dusty, or going out to the hayfield with Dad, or feeding the calves, or putting the cows in...

"You could wear your hair in a ponytail," Mom said.

"How much more—OUCH!—do you have left?"

"I'm half through."

Lovely. Only halfway.

"Well," Mom inquired, "what about the ponytail? Then your hair wouldn't fly all over the place."

"But I don't like wearing a ponytail," I said, reaching up to rub the spot where my mother had most recently yanked out a snarl.

"Why not?" she asked.

"OWWWW!!"

"Can't you yell quieter?" Mom said. "You make it sound like I'm trying to murder you."

I was wondering how someone was supposed to yell more quietly when my big sister came downstairs.

"How did I know that it was time for you to get your hair done?" Loretta said.

"Would you finish?" Mom asked.

I drew in a deep breath and let it out slowly. The difference between Loretta combing my hair and Mom combing my hair was like the difference between coughing once and coming down with a full-blown case of pneumonia.

I'd never had pneumonia, but the grandmother of one of my friends at school had gotten pneumonia during the winter, and according to my friend, it wasn't any fun at all.

Loretta sat down in another kitchen chair, so I went over and sat down on the floor in front of her.

"It's really snarly tonight," Loretta said, as she began working at the knots.

My sister lifted the long hair off the back of my neck, held it one hand and with the other hand, began to comb from the bottom up.

"I know it's snarly," I said. "It was windy out today, and when Dad took the four-sixty over to the other place to bring the hay conditioner home, he asked if I wanted to ride with him. So I did."

"Oh," Loretta said, "you were out in two kinds of wind—wind from the sky and wind from the tractor."

"Daddy wanted to bring the conditioner home because he didn't think he'd need it anymore this year," I said.

The hay conditioner was a piece of equipment with rollers that squeezed the water out of the hay right after it was cut so the hay would dry faster. Dad had taken the hay conditioner to the other place when he started to cut second crop hay, but because it had not rained much lately, he said the hay wasn't juicy enough to waste the time and the gasoline using the conditioner.

"What else did you do today?" Loretta asked as she continued working at the snarls in my hair.

"We checked on the blackberries this afternoon," I said.

"And will there be any?" Loretta asked.

I started to nod and then remembered I ought to keep my head still. "I think so," I said. "There's lots of green ones. Dad said if it doesn't rain soon, though, they'll be small and seedy."

Loretta let go of my hair and gathered up one side to comb it from the other direction.

"I suppose we'll just have to wait and see about the blackberries," she said. "So that was it? You rode over to the other place on the tractor with Dad and you checked on the blackberries?"

"Dusty and I went back to get the cows tonight," I said. "And, oh—I rode my bike down to see Mrs. Paulson this morning."

"And how was Hannah?" Loretta inquired.

"Good," I said. "Except her knees hurt today."

Twenty minutes later, my sister finished combing out the snarls.

In the meantime, Mom had gone into the living room to work on an embroidery project. The fall bazaar for our church was still four months away, but she said she wanted to embroider as much as she could so it would be ready for the church to sell by the time the bazaar arrived.

I went into the living room and sat down in the rocking chair.

"You never did answer my question about why you won't wear a ponytail," Mom said as she snipped off a bit of thread.

"My hair gets wrapped around the rubber band," I said. "Remember?"

Last week, because Mom insisted, I had worn a ponytail, and then that evening, after trying all kinds of ways to get the rubber band out, she ended up cutting it out.

I wasn't sure which was worse—Mom combing my hair or Mom pulling out a rubber band.

"Maybe you should get your hair cut," my mother said.

I turned to stare at her.

"But—all the other girls in school have long hair!" I said.

Which wasn't strictly true, of course. A couple of girls in my grade wore their hair short.

"And I suppose if all the other girls jumped off a bridge, you'd do it too?" Mom said, looking up from her embroidery.

Whenever I brought up the 'everybody else' argument, Mom always came back with 'the bridge.'

"I have an idea about how to keep the snarls out," Loretta said.

She sat down on the davenport and looked back and forth between Mom and me.

"It's this stuff I've seen advertised that if you spray it on your hair when you wash it, it's supposed to keep it from getting so tangled," my sister explained.

"Do you think it works?" Mom asked.

"Only one way to know for sure," Loretta said. "I'll see if I can find some tomorrow after work."

The next evening when my sister came home, she handed me a small paper bag.

"I found the spray stuff," Loretta said. "And I also found some hair bands. They're made out of elastic so your hair won't get wound around them."

"When can I wash my hair so we can see if it works?" I asked.

The daily routine of getting my hair brushed was bad enough, but the tangles were even worse if my hair was wet.

"What about tonight when you're done helping Dad out in the barn?" my mother said.

Later in the evening, after we were finished with the chores, Loretta helped me wash my hair in the kitchen sink, and then she wrapped a big, white bath towel around my head.

"Your hair will have to stay wrapped up for fifteen minutes so it's not dripping wet," Loretta said. "Let's go outside for a while."

To the west, where the sun had almost dropped to the horizon, thin clouds caught the slanting rays and glowed yellow-orange, as if someone had lit a candle behind the clouds.

I had never seen clouds like that, and we watched until the brilliant yellow-orange had faded away. After that, we went to look at the roses.

Loretta had planted two rose bushes in the yard. One was red and one was yellow. The red roses smelled heavenly sweet, but the yellow roses were sweeter yet.

My sister broke off one of the yellow roses and a couple of red rose buds. When we went back inside, she put the roses into a vase and set the vase in the middle of the table. By then it was time for her to comb out my hair. She unwrapped the towel from my head, spritzed my hair with the tangles spray, and worked it in with her fingers.

"Are you ready?" she asked as she picked up a comb.

I nodded and gritted my teeth, prepared for the worst, and...

It was like magic.

The comb slid through my hair and did not snag on a single strand.

"Well," Mom said as she watched from her chair by the kitchen table. "Imagine that."

"There's just one catch, though," Loretta said.

"What's the catch?" Mom asked.

"It only works on wet hair," Loretta said.

I spun around to look at my sister. "What?" I said.

"It only works on wet hair," she repeated.

During the few minutes Loretta had been combing my hair, I had been busy imagining how nice it would be when Mom combed my hair after a long day of me running around the farm.

"I guess that means we're still going to have problems when it's time to comb out her hair in the morning and at night," Mom said.

"I think so," Loretta said. She turned to me. "I'm sorry. I was really hoping it would work on dry hair, too."

The next morning when Mom combed out my hair, I thought it was possible that it was not *quite* as snarled, although I had little time to think about it.

"Let's try a ponytail and see how the hair bands work," Mom said.

Before I could say anything, she started to gather my hair together.

Although I thought I was ready, when my mother slipped the elastic band over the ponytail and—pulled—for a second there, I wondered if she had pulled the whole ponytail right off my head.

"Does it have to be this tight?" I said as I stood up.

The mirror hanging on the wall by the kitchen sink was only a few feet away, but I was afraid to look in the mirror because I figured my face would be stretched back from my nose and that my eyes would have been stretched into slits.

"For Heaven's sake, it's not *that* tight," Mom said. "And it will loosen up as the day goes on, I'm sure."

In the evening, when my mother was ready to take the ponytail out, the elastic band slid out my hair with no problem.

"See?" Mom said, "I told you a ponytail was a good idea."

While it was true that the elastic band had come right out on the first try, I still was not convinced about the ponytail. Even though the hair band was gone, my hair still thought it was in a ponytail. Instead of lying flat, it stayed bunched up.

"Why did you have to make it so *tight*?" I complained.

"Oh, don't be silly," Mom said. "It wasn't *that* terrible. Must you dramatize everything so much?"

"What does that mean? Dramatize?"

"It means you play everything for all it's worth," she said.

While I was considering what *that* meant and deciding it probably wasn't good, Mom spoke up again.

"Besides, if you think I'm bad with a ponytail, you should have had my mother braid your hair," Mom replied. "She made braids so tight they'd stick straight out."

There it was again.

Grandma Inga.

"I thought you said she was a tiny woman," I said.

"She was," Mom said. "It didn't take me very long to grow taller than my mother. And like I always say, she probably didn't weigh a hundred pounds soaking wet."

"That's right," Dad said. "Inga was a little bit of a thing."

My father had just come in from the barn.

"So what's this about Inga?" he asked as he sat down in his chair at the end of the table.

My mother drew a deep breath and blew it out quickly. It was a sound, I knew, that meant she was exasperated.

"Every time I do something with her hair, she complains that I'm too rough," Mom said. "If she thinks *I'm* bad, she should have had my mother comb her hair."

"If Grandma Inga was so tiny, then how could she be this strong?" I said, turning around and pointing to the bunch of hair that still thought it was in a ponytail.

I turned back to look at Mom.

Dad grinned. "Yup, Inga was tiny. Not tall like your Ma. Your mother takes after her Pa. And Inga didn't have polio, either, so that musta made a difference."

"That's right," my mother said. "She didn't have polio."

"And since she didn't have polio, she didn't spend all day leaning on things to keep her balance and to hold herself up," my father said.

Mom looked at Dad with narrowed eyes. "What's that got to do with it?"

"Inga had small hands and arms, too, not like Ma," Dad said.

My mother looked down at her hands and arms—looked back at Dad—and then down at her hands and arms.

"Are you trying to tell me that because I push my entire weight up out of a chair about twenty times a day that I'm stronger than I think I am?" Mom said.

Dad lifted one shoulder in a slight shrug.

My mother stared at him for several seconds, threw her hands up into the air and let them fall on her lap.

"Ha-ha," she chortled. "Ha-ha-ha. Hee-hee. Ha-ha-ha-ha!"

She shook her head. "I'm—ha-ha!— stronger than I think I am."

"It is not," I said, drawing myself up to my full height, "very funny."

Mom turned in my direction. Her face was crumpled with laughter and her blue eyes were swimming with tears. She held my gaze, blinked—and then bit her lips.

"No," she said at last, wiping the tears out of her eyes. "Now that I think about it, you're right. It's not very funny. All this time you've been complaining about me pulling your hair when I comb it, and I never gave it a thought. I suppose I *am* stronger than I think am."

"Mom?" I said. "Why can't I comb my own hair?"

"Do you think you can get the snarls out?" Mom asked.

"I can try," I said. "And then maybe at night, Loretta could comb it."

"Sounds like a good idea," Dad said. "The kiddo ought to be able to comb her own hair. She combs Dusty's hair and that's awful bad for tangles sometimes."

"Yes, well, she uses a curry comb on Dusty," Mom said.

"Hey! I could use—"

Before I finished my sentence, Mom cut me off. "Don't even think about it," she said.

It was too late, of course. I had already thought about it—and had decided it wouldn't work. When I combed Dusty's mane and tail with the currycomb, I pulled out some of her hair. The clumps were like the snarls Mom combed out of my hair.

I felt bad about pulling Dusty's hair, but Dad said it was okay because Dusty had such thick hair and that horses didn't have feeling in their mane and tail, anyway. At first I thought he was making it up, but when Dad wrapped a strand of Dusty's hair around his finger and pulled it out, she never blinked, so then I knew it was true.

Horses, it seemed to me, were extremely lucky. I had no idea what it would be like not to have any feeling in the roots of my hair.

Wish I did, though.

~ 14 ~
Much Too Close...

I hung up the telephone and headed for the kitchen where Mom was washing the dinner dishes. The kitchen window was open, and in the distance, from the field at the back of the farm by the big pine trees, I could hear the 460 Farmall. Dad was cutting hay.

"What did Vicki want?" Mom asked as she rinsed a plate.

Vicki was my best friend. We were the same age, although she was taller than me. Her family had lived on the turkey farm a mile and a half from our farm for a couple of years, but it still seemed like a miracle that I had a friend who lived so close.

"Oh, nothing," I said. "Not much of anything. Not really."

"She wants you to come over this afternoon, doesn't she?"

I almost dropped the plate I was drying. "How did you know?"

"I've got ears. I could hear your half of the conversation," Mom said.

"Oh," I said, as I put the plate in the cupboard. "Well? Can I go over to Vicki's house this afternoon?

"Can I?" Mom said.

"I mean, may I?"

One of these days, I was hoping that I would remember to ask by saying 'may I' without Mom having to remind me. "Of course you are capable of doing what you are asking," she sometimes said. "But the real question is—do you have permission?"

My mother finished washing another plate and handed it to me.

"Dad's cutting hay right now, there's nothing ready to bale—so, yes, you have my permission to go over to Vicki's house this afternoon," Mom said.

A few minutes later, when the dishes were finished and my mother had headed into the living room to embroider, I got my bike out of the machine shed. I wished I could have ridden Dusty, but the bike was faster, and besides, I didn't want my pony to get hot and sweaty. The thermometer by the kitchen window said it was eighty-eight degrees, and when I rode Dusty to the hayfield on a hot, humid day, often she would be dripping wet with sweat when we got there.

Dad said it was because my little brown pony was plump and because ponies had thicker hair than horses.

When I arrived at Vicki's house twenty minutes later, my friend was waiting out in the front yard. Although I was sweating a little, I didn't feel too hot. Some of the trip to Vicki's house was uphill, but some of it was downhill, too, and when I coasted downhill, I got a chance to cool off.

"What are we going to do this afternoon?" I asked as I put the kickstand down on my bike.

"Let's explore the woods," Vicki said. "It's shady in the big woods. Maybe we'll find some raspberries!"

A short distance from the house was a woods of large pine trees. If Vicki and I linked hands on one side, we could almost touch hands on the other sides of the trunks. Dad said they were white pine. The trees were so big and made so much shade that hardly any brush grew beneath them. But in a few places where the trees were farther apart, wild raspberries grew in the open spots.

"I know!" I said. "Let's ride our bikes."

A dirt road went past the barn and directly to the white pine woods, and in no time at all, we parked our bikes in the shade of one of the big trees.

"Doesn't it smell good?" Vicki said.

I stopped and drew a deep breath. The woods smelled sweet with the scent of pine pitch warmed by the sun. Underneath the branches of the large pine trees, the air felt cooler. Crickets chirped in the long grass beside the road, and from among the branches above our heads, a squirrel chattered. Not far away, a chipmunk sat on a fallen branch, watching us.

"Hey!" Vicki exclaimed. "I just had a *great* idea!"

"What?" I said.

"Let's go camping!"

"Camping?"

Vicki's family went on vacations during the summer, and when they went on vacation, they often went camping. I had never been on a vacation. My family did not take vacations. Dad said he had too much farm work to do. I had never been camping, either.

"I don't know why I didn't think of it before," Vicki said. "We've got a tent. And sleeping bags. And a camp stove—if Mom will let us use it. And we've got lanterns, and well, all kinds of stuff."

"But where would we *go* camping?" I asked.

Vicki spread her arms wide. "Right here, of course. In the big woods."

I looked around. Just beyond where the road ended was an open area beneath the trees that seemed like it might be big enough to set up a tent, especially if we cut down a few bushes by the road.

"Do you really think your mom will let you?" I asked, turning toward my friend.

"Sure, why not," she replied. "What about your mom, though?"

"She *might* say it's okay," I said.

I looked at Vicki and she looked at me. And then we both grinned, hopped on our bikes and headed back to the house.

Minutes later, we were standing in the kitchen.

"Hmmmm," Vicki's mom said. "Camping. And you want to go right in the woods here?"

She got up, poured a cup of coffee and came back to the table.

"I guess I don't see why not," she said. "You'll be close to the house. So yes, you can go camping if you want to. But you'd better ask your dad if it's okay to use the tent."

"Where is Dad?" Vicki asked.

"The last time I saw him, he was on his way out to the barn to see if he could get that other tractor started."

Sure enough, when we walked into the barn, a long white building that wasn't used for anything now except storage, Vicki's dad was tinkering with the tractor.

"Camping?" he said. "In the woods right here? And you want to use the tent?"

"And the camp stove, if we could. And the lanterns. And sleeping bags," Vicki said.

"Boy, you kids don't ask for much, do you," he said.

"Please Dad?" Vicki said.

He grinned suddenly. "Yes, you can use the camping equipment. When you decide you're going, I'll even haul everything out there for you. And if you want to leave the tent set up for a week or two so you can camp out a couple of times, that's all right, too."

He selected a wrench from the toolbox on the floor. "What are the pruning shears for?" he asked.

On our way to the barn, we had stopped at the garage. Vicki had rummaged around on the workbench until she found the pruning shears, which looked like a big scissors with a hook at the end.

"We're going to cut some bushes at our campsite," Vicki said.

"Be careful with those," Vicki's dad said, turning toward the tractor. "If the shears can cut off a small tree branch, it can cut off your fingers, too."

"Yes, Dad," Vicki said.

We went back out to our campsite and cut down the bushes by the road to make more room for the tent. The day was still hot, but since the sun had moved farther west, our campsite was now completely in the shade. After we had finished piling up the bushes, it was time for me to go home.

"Ask your mom right away and then call me," Vicki said.

All the way home, I thought about how I should ask to go camping. But even as I pushed my bicycle up the hill of our driveway, I still didn't know what to say.

"You're home, I see," Mom said as I walked into the house. "Just in time to put the cows in."

I went to the cupboard, pulled out a glass and filled it with cold water. Before the glass was full, I decided I might as well jump right in and ask.

"Mom," I said, after I had drunk half the glass, "can I—errr—I mean—*may* I go camping?"

"Camping?" my mother said. "Where?"

"In the woods by Vicki's house," I said.

"When?" Mom asked.

"I don't know for sure," I said. "Sometime this summer."

"For how long?" she asked.

I shrugged. "Maybe just for one night. Or two."

"Well," Mom said. "I suppose it would be all right. You'll be close to the house there. Just as long you don't plan on going when we've got haying to do."

My mother was sitting in her chair at the end of the kitchen table. I set down my glass and threw my arms around her shoulders.

"Don't hug me so hard," Mom said, her voice muffled against my shoulder. "I can't breathe."

I let go of my mother and went back to the sink for another glass of water. Just then, Dad walked into the house.

"I thought you were still out in the field," Mom said.

"I put the can on the muffler and left the tractor back there," Dad said. "We'll need it again soon anyway. So why waste the gas driving it up to the shed?"

When Dad left the 460 Farmall out in the field, he put a tin can over the muffler.

"How much hay did you cut?" Mom asked.

"That's why I came home. I didn't want to cut more than we can bale in a day. It won't rain tonight, I don't think. But it probably will in a couple of days. It's awfully hot and it's starting to get humid."

"Mom?" I said. "Is it okay if I call Vicki now?"

"Now?" Mom said.

"Just to tell her I got permission to go camping. Then I'll go out and help Dad put the cows in."

"Well, as long as you don't talk for more than a few minutes, all right," she said.

When I told Vicki that Mom said I could go camping, her squeal of happy delight made my eardrum hurt.

The next afternoon, Vicki called right after dinner, and we decided that we should spend our first night in the tent the following evening.

On the afternoon of the 'big camping trip'—that's what Mom called it, 'the big camping trip'—Dad and I baled and unloaded two loads of hay before Ingman came home from work at the creamery a little after three o'clock. Then Dad and Ingman baled the last two loads out in the field, and while they were doing that, I put the cows in the barn and fed them. Dad parked the two loads of hay in the pole shed and said we could unload them later.

All day yesterday and today, the wind had been blowing out of the southeast. The church was south of our farm, I knew, and the Paulson's farm was east. The wind was blowing halfway between the church and our neighbor's place, so I knew it was out of the southeast. When we went one direction on the hayfield, the wind had cooled my face, and when we went the other way, it had cooled my back.

But now, as evening approached, the wind was beginning to die down, and with a calmer wind, the air felt hot and sticky. It was as if I were trying to breathe through a warm, wet, wool blanket.

"When we're finished eating supper, you'd better have Loretta take you over to Vicki's so you can get your tent set up before dark," Dad said as we walked back to the house for supper. "I bet you're gonna sleep good in the tent tonight. It'll be cooler there than it will be in the house."

After supper, I put my camping gear in a large cardboard box: an extra blanket that Vicki said I would need to put on the floor of the tent underneath the sleeping bag, my pillow, two bottles of orange soda pop, a bag of potato chips, two apples, two bananas, a dozen of the oatmeal cookies that my sister had baked, my pajamas, and an extra pair of socks.

"Before you get too carried away here, hold on just a minute," Mom said. "I want to talk to you."

I turned to look at my mother.

"What are you going to do if it rains tonight?" she asked.

"They'll be in the tent. They won't get wet," Dad said.

"That's not what I meant," Mom said. "What I meant is—what are you going to do if storms?"

"Is it going to storm?" I said.

A sinking feeling in the pit of my stomach made me feel suddenly queasy. A little thunder rumbling in the distance was one thing. But a big thunderstorm was quite another. I was not especially fond of thunder and lightning—not since the time when we'd had a horrendous thunderstorm and a bolt of lightning had struck close to the house.

Before the roar of the thunder died away, a blue fireball had leaped out one of the electrical outlets in the living room and had rolled around on the floor until it fizzled out. Before I knew what was happening, another bolt of lightning had struck close to the house and another blue fireball had leaped out of the socket. My mother and big sister had both screamed loud enough to make the hair stand up on the back of my neck.

"*Is* it going to storm?" I repeated.

"Maybe," Dad said. "It's been hot enough."

"So, what *are* you going to do if it storms?" Mom said.

"Won't we be safe in the tent?" I asked.

"Not if it's windy enough to blow one of the trees down on top of the tent," Dad said.

"Oh," I said.

"I want to know if you have a plan in case it storms," my mother said.

"We're only a little ways from the house," I said. "If we hear that it's starting to thunder, we'll just go to the house right away."

My mother looked at me intently. "Are you sure that's what you'll do?"

"Of course that's what they'll do," Dad said. "They're neither one of 'em stupid. You worry too much, Ma."

My big sister cleared her throat. "In this case, I think she's right to worry. But if they're only a little ways from the house, I'm sure they'll be fine."

"Yes, Mom," I said. "We'll be fine. We'll go to the house right away if it's thundering."

"Okay. That's what I wanted to know," Mom said.

I carried my cardboard box out to Loretta's car, and then we were ready to leave. When Loretta pulled into the driveway at Vicki's, my friend came down the steps to meet us.

"Let's take your box in the house. We can put the food in the cooler. And we can put the rest of my stuff in your box," Vicki said.

"Have fun!" Loretta said. She started the car, waved, and drove around the circle driveway back to the road.

Once we were inside the house, Vicki opened the cooler. She had put two plastic bags filled with ice cubes in the bottom. In addition to my two bottles of soda pop, the apples, the bananas and the cookies were two more bottles of soda pop, two candy bars, more cookies, two pears, a dozen eggs, a loaf of bread, a package of hotdogs, a package of hotdog buns, a bottle of ketchup and a bottle of mustard.

"When we get our stuff unloaded and get the sleeping bags set up, we can explore the woods, and then later, we can eat supper," Vicki said.

"I already ate supper," I said.

"Me, too," Vicki replied. "But we can eat again, can't we?"

Between the two of us, we lugged the cooler out to the back step. Vicki's dad had backed his pickup truck around by the garage. He was going to haul our camping gear out to the campsite.

"The tent's already set up," Vicki explained. "Dad helped me do that this afternoon."

"What have you got in here? Rocks?" her dad asked, as he lifted the big cooler to put it in the truck.

"No, Dad," Vickie said. "Just some ice. Our food. And pop, too."

He went back to the step and lifted the cardboard box. "This is more like it," he said. "What's in here?"

"That's our blankets, pillows, pajamas and—what else?" Vicki said.

"Potato chips and cookies," I said. There was no room in the cooler for the potato chips and the cookies.

"At least we won't have to worry about you kids getting hungry," Vicki's father remarked.

Before he opened the driver's door, he stopped to wipe the sweat off his forehead. "Sure is sticky out here tonight, isn't it," he said.

The bumpy ride to the campsite was over almost before it started. If the barn hadn't been built where it was, we probably would have been able to see the tent from the back steps of the house.

Vicki's dad put the cooler and the cardboard box on the ground underneath a tree right next to the tent.

As he turned to get in the truck, he stopped. "Are you sure you're going to be all right out here? What if it storms?"

"Yes, Dad," Vickie said. "We'll be fine."

"If it starts to thunder, we'll come back to the house right away," I said.

Vicki looked at me with eyebrows raised.

Her dad nodded. "The house isn't very far. I think you'll be all right."

He got into the pickup and shut the door. "Have fun!" he said as he started to turn the truck around.

"Why did you say we'd go back to the house if it starts to thunder?" Vicki asked after her dad had driven away, leaving a cloud of dust from the sandy road hanging in the evening air.

"I said we'd go back to the house because my mom wanted to know what we'd do if it stormed, and that's what I told her," I explained.

"I get it," Vicki said.

After we had unpacked everything and had arranged the sleeping bags inside the tent, we headed into the woods. The sun would not set for another hour, giving us plenty of daylight to do some exploring.

During the next hour, we crawled over logs and fought our way through pockets of brush. We found a bird's nest that had fallen to the ground. And we saw a big snake slithering through the pine needles. It was a brownish colored snake, and it was bigger than the bull snake I had seen by the granary one time.

When we returned to the tent, darkness had begun to settle into the woods. Vicki lit the lantern so we could see and the camp stove so we could cook our second supper for the night. Grilled hotdogs, potato chips and soda pop had never tasted quite so good, in my opinion, although now that the sun had set, the mosquitoes had come out. In between bites of hot dog, I slapped at mosquitoes landing on my arms.

"Did you bring any bug spray?" Vicki asked.

I shook my head.

"Me, neither," she said.

When we were finished eating, we put the rest of the food back into the cooler, closed the cover, and then we took the lantern with us and went into the tent. We put on our pajamas, crawled into the sleeping bags—and talked and giggled and laughed until Vicki figured she'd better blow out the lantern before we fell asleep with it still burning.

I have no idea how long we were asleep, but suddenly, we were both sitting bolt upright.

"What was that?" I asked, as Vickie reached for the flashlight she had left near her sleeping bag.

The words were no more out of my mouth when a bright flash of lightning was almost simultaneously accompanied by a clap of thunder.

"That was close," Vickie muttered. "Do you think it hit a tree?"

I shrugged. "Maybe."

Before I could suggest we ought to make a run for the house, lightning flickered again followed by a loud *Ka-CRASH.*

In the circle of light cast by the flashlight, I could see that Vicki was as wide-eyed as I felt.

"Wanna go to the house?" she asked. But then she shook her head. Neither of us felt much like venturing outside.

Another bolt of lightning flashed, but before we could cover our ears, the thunder hit. And then we heard another sound, like the sound wood made when Dad split apart blocks with the ax to make smaller chunks for the woodstove…

"Was that a tree?" Vicki wondered.

"Or maybe just a branch," I said.

The silver maples around our yard occasionally lost a branch during a thunderstorm. Branches fell to the ground with such force that they sometimes left dents in the lawn.

"What if it had hit the tent?" Vicki said.

Before I could say anything, we heard yet another sound—as if someone were dumping buckets of water over the tent.

It was raining.

One second, it was not raining—and then the next second, it was.

And not only was it raining, but the sides of the tent were moving in and out—in and out—as if the tent were breathing.

"What's that?" I asked.

"Wind," Vicki said. "It's getting windy."

Vicki set the flashlight down and stood up to look through one of the little window openings near the ceiling. While she was standing there, lightning sizzled again followed immediately by a crack of thunder.

Vicki turned from the window and, in one leap, landed on her sleeping bag and quickly crawled inside.

"Now what are we going to do?" she said.

"I don't know," I said. "

Lightning sizzled once again, followed immediately by another *Ka-Crash!*—and then came a strange creaking sound.

"What's that?" I said.

The creaking grew louder, and then—*ka-thump!*—right next to the tent.

"I think that was another tree," Vicki said in a tiny little voice.

"Or a branch," I said.

Lightning sizzled yet again followed immediately by another *Ka-boom!*

The rain also was still falling in buckets.

Then, in spite of the lightning and the thunder and the rain, I became aware of a different sound—sort of a rhythmic humming.

"What's that?" I said.

"What's what?" Vicki asked, cocking her head to the side.

"Sounds like—" I said.

"Look!" Vicki pointed toward the front of the tent. The whole tent lit up when lightning flashed, but this was a different light. It wasn't coming from above, it was coming straight at us.

"It's a car!" Vicki said, throwing back the top part of her sleeping bag. She rushed to the window. "It *is* a car!" she said. "It's my mom!"

I put my shoes on and so did Vicki.

"I'm going to unzip one side of the door. But not all the way up," she said. "You get out and run for the car. I'll be right behind you, after I close the zipper again."

As soon as I got out of the tent, I ran straight for the car. The windshield wipers slapped back and forth and back and forth, and when I had almost reached the car, Vicki's mom unlatched the door and pushed it open toward me. I leaped in and slid across the seat, and seconds later, Vicki leaped in the car behind me and slammed the door shut.

"Look at how wet you are!" Vicki's mom yelled above the sound of the rain pelting on the car roof. The rain had been loud in the tent. It was almost deafening in the car.

My hair was dripping wet and so was Vicki's. Our pajamas were soaked as well. Vicki's mom turned the car around, and after we reached the house, she drove into the garage and parked, and from there, we ran the few steps to the back door.

Later on, after we had changed into dry clothes, we crawled into bed in Vicki's room. Rain was still falling at a steady rate. We could hear it on the roof above our heads.

"Some camping trip," I said. "We didn't even get to sleep in the tent for one night!"

"I know," Vicki said. "But that's okay. When everything dries out, we can try it again."

Neither of us said anything for a few minutes.

"You know what?" Vicki said.

"What?"

"After we asked Mom about going camping, after you went home, that is, I asked if we could go down by the lake."

The lake, although not far away, was farther away from the house than the woods. Maybe as far away as the church was from our house, and that, I knew, was a half a mile.

"The lake!" I said.

"I thought the woods was too close to the house. I thought it wouldn't seem like camping," Vicki said. "Mom and I got in a fight about it, too."

"You did?"

"Just a little one," Vicki said. "She said she knew best and that if we wanted to go camping, we would have to go close to the house. At least for the first couple of times."

A minute later, Vicki turned out the light, and as I laid there in the dark with my eyes closed, all I could think about were the brilliant, sizzling flashes of lightning, the crash of the thunder, and the ominous creaking and splintering sounds.

The next morning when we woke up, the sun was shining, and before Dad came to get me, we went out to the campsite. A big branch off one of the pine trees lay on the ground only a few feet from the tent. But as I looked at it more closely, I realized it wasn't really a branch—it was more like half the tree.

"That was kind of close," Vicki said.

"Too close," I said.

"It's sort of funny, in a way," Vicki said, "because I thought this was *too close* to the house for camping."

"Yeah," I said, "but it seemed awful far away last night."

I looked at Vicki and she looked at me—and then we both looked at the tree.

"Well," Vicki said. "It's like my dad says, 'almost only counts in hand grenades and horseshoes.'"

"Hey!" I said. "My dad says that, too."

Which was true. If I said I almost fell off Dusty, or I almost fell off my bike, or I almost dropped a hammer on my toe, he would say 'almost doesn't count except in hand grenades and horseshoes.'

"When should we try camping again?" I asked.

"How about Friday night?" Vicki said.

"Okay," I said.

Over the next two weeks, all together, we camped out in the tent for five nights.

But never again did the house seem too close—or too far away.

No, actually—it was just right.

~ 15 ~
Up North

For several weeks, Dad had been planning a trip up north to pick blueberries. "The first nice Sunday when it's not too hot, we'll go," he'd said. And today was the day, now that Mom, Loretta and I were home from church and had changed our clothes.

The sky was a deep, cloudless blue and the air was so clear that every white clover blossom in the lawn—every purple and white petunia around the light pole in the front yard—every leaf on the silver maples—seemed to glitter in the sunlight. I stood beside the car and waited for my mother to make her way down the porch steps, her crutches clicking each time she moved one forward.

As soon as Mom had settled herself in the car and Dad had come back from checking the stock tank to make sure the cows had enough water to last until we came home later this afternoon, Loretta and I climbed in the back seat. And then we were ready to go.

"Have we got everything?" Dad asked.

"I think so," Loretta said.

"The berry pails are in the trunk, and so is our picnic lunch," Mom said.

"And we've got lemonade to drink," I chimed in.

Dad started the car. He backed around by the garage, and we headed down the driveway.

For two hours, we drove north. The landscape changed from farm fields to pine woods, and just about the time I thought I was going to starve to death, we arrived at a meadow with pine trees all around it.

"Should we eat now or wait?" Dad asked.

"Let's eat now!" I said. "I'm starving to death."

"I hardly think you're starving to *death*," Mom said. "But now would be a good time for our picnic."

In the trunk of the car sat a cardboard box which held bologna and cheese sandwiches, cucumbers and carrots from our garden, bottles of soda pop that we had bought at the little country store a mile and a half from our farm, some of Loretta's homemade peanut butter cookies and the lemonade she had made this morning. Last night, Dad had taken two plastic pails, filled them to half with water, and then he had put them in the big freezer in the machine shed. The pails of ice were in the box to help keep our food cold.

Mom opened her door and turned sideways in the car until her feet were resting on the ground. Dad opened his door, Loretta and I each opened our doors, and with a cool breeze blowing through the car, we ate our picnic lunch.

When we were finished, it was time to pick blueberries.

Dad had known of this spot for years, but even though he hadn't been here to pick blueberries in a long time, he was pretty sure there would be plenty.

I had never been picking blueberries before. When we went to the restaurant in town while we were waiting for our pickup load of corn and oats to be made into cow feed at the feed mill, I always asked for blueberry pie.

We headed toward the meadow, Dad in front, Loretta following Dad and me following Loretta.

"Look at 'em all," Dad said, as he waded into a thicket of knee-high bushes. "They're just loaded. We'll get as many as we want, and then some."

"Oh, good, I can make a blueberry pie!" Loretta said, as she followed Dad into the thicket. My sister was wearing a pair of pink and white slacks, a short-sleeved white blouse and a blue bandana tied over her dark, curly hair.

Everywhere I looked, the bushes were covered with blueberries as big around as the end of my finger. Loretta and Dad each carried five-quart plastic ice cream pails, but Dad had given me a container he had made from a one-pound coffee can. The little berry pail had a wire handle, and it was the same kind of pail we used for picking blackberries. When I picked blackberries, I tied the pail to my belt loops so I could use both hands.

A cool breeze out of the north fanned my face and arms as I sat down on the ground by the first clump of bushes. I could never sit down while I picked blackberries because the brambles were too prickly. But here I could reach right around me until I ran out of berries.

I had already covered the bottom of the pail when Dad spoke up.

"Where's the kiddo?" he said.

"Here I am!" I said, popping up from my spot in the blueberry bushes.

Dad laughed. "Sittin' down on the job, are ya? Getting any blueberries? Or are you eating them all?"

"No," I said, tipping my can toward him. "I'm not eating any. See?"

I had, in fact, eaten some when I first started. The blueberries smelled so good, and were such a deep, delicious blue, I could not resist. Fresh blueberries, I discovered, tasted as good as fresh blackberries.

Before I sat down again, I paused to look around. The ring of dark green pine trees stood out against a sky that was now decorated with puffy white clouds. The wind sighing through the pine boughs and birds twittering from the treetops were the only sounds I could hear. No cars. No machinery. No barking dogs. Nothing at all to spoil the afternoon.

Well, nothing except for one little black insect crawling on my leg below the hem of my shorts.

About the size of an ant, the bug did not look like an ant. It was more round than that, and it had different kinds of legs. I tried to brush the insect off, but it would not brush off, so I picked it off with my fingernails. I tried to let go of the bug, but I could not because the pesky thing kept crawling along my fingers. I finally got rid of it by wiping my hand on the ground.

I was going to start picking blueberries again, but even though I knew the insect was gone, I could not get over the idea that it was *not* gone. I kept remembering the way it had felt when it crawled on my bare leg.

Every couple of minutes I stopped picking blueberries to check for another insect like the first one. But after a while when I did not find any more, I forgot about it and concentrated on filling my pail.

Bit by bit, the blueberries piled up in the little one-pound coffee can, covering the first ring and then the second. Filling the whole can seemed like a big job, but filling the can up to one ring and then the next did not seem like much work at all.

A couple of times during the afternoon, I went to the car to drink some lemonade and to talk to Mom, who said she was having fun watching the clouds make different shapes. "It's been a long time since I've sat outside and watched clouds," she said.

The sun was still high in the sky when Dad announced that we should start for home so we would arrive in time to feed the cows and do the evening milking.

On the way home, once again I sat in the back seat with my big sister, and as we drove through evergreen forests and marshes with tall, green grass, it seemed to me that the whole day had been perfect. The sun had been warm but not too hot, and a breeze had cooled my face when I turned into the wind. But best of all, we had picked four five-quart pails of blueberries and half of another pail. Plenty of blueberries for my cereal and for dishes of blueberries with cream and sugar—and for Loretta to make blueberry pie—and for Mom to freeze blueberries so we could have pie during the winter.

It wasn't until a few days later that I began to wonder if the trip up north really had been quite so perfect.

I had come in from the barn, and Mom had decided she ought to brush my hair. Sometimes I was able to brush my own hair. But not today. It was too tangled. Ever since my mother realized she was stronger that what she thought from leaning on the furniture to get around, she had been a tiny bit better about not pulling so hard while she combed my hair.

Even at that, while Mom yanked and tugged, each minute seemed more like ten. So, when she abruptly stopped brushing, I didn't bother to wonder why but instead drew a deep breath and let it out slowly.

My sense of relief lasted only a few seconds.

"*Yeeeeeek!*" Mom screeched. "What *is* that?"

"What's what?" I asked, putting my hand up to the back of my hair.

Mom tapped my wrist with the brush. "Don't touch it."

"Don't touch what?"

Loretta, hurried over to look at the spot where Mom pointed.

"*Eeeeeeek!*" my sister shrieked.

I had no idea what all the yelling was about—but I knew it could not be anything good.

"What's wrong?" I asked. "What's the matter?"

"Ummm, uhhhh," Mom stuttered. "It's…it's nothing. Nothing at all."

"That's right," my sister said in a soothing tone of voice. "Don't worry—it's nothing."

What *were* they talking about?

"It's nothing?"

"Don't worry?"

Mom had tapped my hand with the brush and said don't touch 'it.' That in itself seemed like a pretty good reason to worry. Never mind all the yelling.

"Well?" I questioned. "What did you find?"

"It's...ahhhhh," Mom said. "Well, it's ahhhhh, it's a wood tick. I think."

"What's a wood tick?"

"An insect," my sister explained.

An insect? If it was only a bug...

"Pick it off," I said.

A long silence greeted my suggestion.

"We can't," Mom said finally.

"Why not?" I asked.

"Because it's embedded," Loretta said.

"It's em—what'ed?"

"Embedded. It means it's stuck in your skin," Mom explained.

"Stuck?"

"Wood ticks burrow into the skin, and then they suck blood until they get all puffed up," my sister said.

"*Yuck!*" I cried, thoroughly disgusted by the idea of an insect sucking my blood. "Do something!"

"We *will*," Mom said. "Just as soon as we figure out how."

"What do you mean 'how?' Can't you just pull it out?"

To my way of thinking, pulling the wood tick out couldn't hurt any worse than Mom brushing my hair. It was only an insect, after all.

My mother gasped. "Pull it out? Are you crazy?"

"What's wrong with pulling it out?"

"You'll get an infection," my mother replied.

Once I had gotten an infection from a sliver in my finger. Mom tried to dig the sliver out with a needle that she had sterilized in the flame of a match. A little piece remained behind, and in a few days, a small pocket of pus had gathered around it. When Mom squeezed the end of my finger, the pus came out and so did the rest of the sliver.

"How can a bug give me an infection?" I asked.

"If the head breaks off and stays in your skin, that's how," Mom said.

Well, okay, so maybe pulling the tick out wasn't such a good idea. A tiny bit of sliver was one thing—but a *whole head*?

"We'll just see if we can get it to back out," Loretta said. "That will be better."

"But what can we use to get it to back out?" Mom asked.

My sister patted her dark, curly hair. "Well, we can try peppermint extract, for one thing. And lemon juice."

"And what about rubbing alcohol?" my mother suggested. "And merthiolate. Oh, and how about vinegar?"

"And we could try some of that salve you've got for burns, too," Loretta said. "It's kind of stinky, so maybe it would work."

"Okay, let's try that then," Mom said.

My sister went upstairs and brought down some of the cotton balls she used to put witch hazel lotion on her face. She soaked a cotton ball in peppermint extract and held the cotton ball to the back of my neck for five minutes.

But when she removed the cotton ball, the wood tick was still firmly in place.

Next she tried lemon juice.

Same thing.

The vinegar didn't work, either.

And neither did the merthiolate.

I was worried about the merthiolate. When I was a very little girl and fell down and skinned my knee, or even now, if I cut myself or got a scratch from the barb wire fence, Mom always brought out the merthiolate. The stuff turned my skin orange—and it burned like fire.

Fortunately, merthiolate on a cotton ball held against the back of my neck did not hurt at all.

After Loretta tried the fingernail polish remover, the only thing that remained was the salve.

"But maybe that will actually work," Mom said. "If the tick is smothered by the salve, it will *have* to let go."

Five minutes later when my sister wiped the salve off the back of my neck, the tick was still firmly in place.

I knew I had been sitting on the floor in front of my mother for a long time, but I did not realize how long until Dad came into the house.

As he walked into the kitchen, I turned my head to look at him and saw his eyebrows inch upwards. Mom and Loretta were bent close to the back of my neck, inspecting the tick.

"What's wrong?" Dad asked.

"Oh, Roy," my mother wailed. "It's an embedded wood tick. She must have gotten it when you were picking blueberries. What in the *world* are we going to do?"

"Do?" Dad asked, sitting down by the table. "You don't have to 'do' anything. Just grab hold of it and pull it out."

My feet had gone numb a few minutes ago and now I could not take it any longer.

"Mom? Would it be all right if I stood up? My feet are numb."

"Your feet—oh, yes. Yes, of course. Stand up," my mother said.

I stood up and slowly walked around the kitchen, trying to work the pins and needles out of my feet.

"I don't see why you're so upset," Dad said. "Just pull the tick out."

My mother turned a fierce gaze in my father's direction.

"Pull it out?" she said. "Won't the head break off?"

He shrugged. "Yeah, it probably will."

"But Dad!" Loretta exclaimed. "What if she gets an infection?"

My father scratched his head. "Nah. I don't think *that* will happen."

"You don't *think*?" Mom said. "But what if it does?"

Sitting on the table were the cotton balls, cotton swabs, the bottle of alcohol, the bottle of lemon juice, the jug of vinegar, the little tin of burn salve, the bottle of peppermint extract—*and* the bottle of fingernail polish remover.

My father looked at all the bottles sitting on the table.

"Is that what you've been putting on it?" he asked.

"We are trying to get it to back out," Mom said.

Dad laughed. "Ticks don't back out. I'm telling you, you've got to pull it out. Besides, if you've been putting alcohol on it—and lemon juice—and vinegar—and fingernail polish remover—and—" He reached over to turn the bottle of peppermint extract so he could see what it was—"and peppermint extract, I doubt she'll get an infection."

"Well..." my mother said.

"How come you know so much about wood ticks, Daddy?"

He glanced at me and winked. "There's always been lots of 'em up north. I've gotten 'em while I was fishing, too."

"You have?"

"And once, when I was just a young sprout, I got a tick in the middle of my back. It was a spot I couldn't get at from neither top nor bottom, so I didn't know it was there."

I felt my eyebrows moving closer together in a frown. "If you didn't know it was there, then how did you know you had a wood tick?"

"Didn't take much to figure that out when I saw the blood on my shirt," he said.

"Blood?"

"Yup. Saw it when I was getting undressed to go to bed. I must have leaned back against something and smashed him."

I suddenly felt sick to my stomach.

Mom and Loretta looked a little green around the gills, too. That's what Mom said when someone looked sick—a little green around the gills.

"But where was the rest of the tick?" I asked.

"Oh, he was still stuck in my back. I asked one of my friends to pull out what was left of him."

"Did you get an infection?" I asked.

Dad shook his head. "Here," he said, standing up and reaching for the pliers he always carried in his pocket, "If you don't want to, I'll pull it out then."

"NO!" my mother and sister cried out in unison.

My father shrugged. "Suit yourself. But the only way it's coming out is if you pull it out."

"We'll use a tweezers," Loretta said. "I've got one upstairs."

"I'm going back outside to shut off the water in the tank and to check the cucumbers to see if they should be picked," Dad said. "Yell if you need me."

My sister went upstairs to get the tweezers and Dad went back outside.

But instead of pulling the tick out, Loretta poked and prodded it with the tip of the tweezers.

"Hey!" she exclaimed after a couple of minutes. "It backed out!"

"It *did?*" Mom said.

"Yes, look, it's right here."

Loretta held up the tweezers with the tick firmly grasped between the two points.

My mother took the tweezers from her.

"I can't begin to tell you how relieved I am," Mom said, as she gingerly laid the dead tick on the table.

I bent closer to get a good look at the thing which had caused so much trouble.

"That's a wood tick?"

"Yes, it is," Mom said, nudging the insect with the tip of her finger.

"But," I said, "I had one of those crawling on my leg when we were picking blueberries."

"You did?" Loretta asked, turning to look at me. "Why didn't you say something?"

"How was I supposed to know that it was a wood tick?"

"No, I guess you wouldn't know, would you," Loretta said.

A minute later, Dad came into the house again.

"Did you get it out?" he asked, as he sat down to take off his shoes.

"Yes, finally," Loretta replied.

"Decided to pull it out, did you?"

"Oh, no," Mom said. "It backed out on its own."

Dad turned to set his shoes by the wall.

"They don't back out," he said, swinging around in his chair. "I've never seen one yet that has. I don't know—maybe they can't. But I'd bet money the head is still in there yet."

Mom and Loretta exchanged glances.

"It backed out," Loretta insisted. "I know it did because I didn't pull it out."

Later on, after Loretta went upstairs and Mom had gone in the living room, Dad asked to see the back of my neck. I went over to him, and I could feel the calloused roughness of his finger touching the spot where the tick had been.

"Is the head in there, do you think?" I asked.

"Yes," Dad said in a low voice. "I think it might be still be in there—because I think it broke off at the head."

I turned to look at him.

"Don't worry," he said. "After all the alcohol and the vinegar and the merthiolate and the fingernail polish remover and the peppermint extract and the lemon juice and whatever else your mother and sister put on there, it won't get infected."

"Do you think we should tell Mom and Loretta?" I asked.

Dad shook his head. "What they don't know won't hurt 'em," he said.

In the end, my father was right. The tick bite did not get infected. My neck was stiff and sore for a week afterward from leaning forward for so long. But the tick bite did not get infected.

And that was almost as good as getting to eat all of the blueberries I wanted with sugar and cream.

Well—not *almost* as good.

Nothing was as good as blueberries with sugar and cream.

~ 16 ~
The Haircut

Already at 6:30 in the morning I could tell it was going to be another hot summer day. When I looked out the upstairs bedroom window, a blue haze hung over the pine trees at the back of the farm. Dad said the blue haze meant the air was humid. The sky had been a hazy blue yesterday morning, too, and in the afternoon, the thin red line on the thermometer had gone up to ninety-four degrees.

After one last look out the bedroom window, I went downstairs and checked the thermometer by the kitchen window. The temperature was seventy degrees—also like yesterday first thing in the morning.

"Do you want me to braid your hair before you go out to the barn?" Mom asked as I turned away from the thermometer. She was sitting by the table with a cup of coffee. "I should have braided your hair yesterday, but I didn't think it was going to be so warm," she added.

"I don't know. Maybe," I said.

I went to the cupboard by the sink, pulled out a glass and turned on the tap. Drinking a glass of water would give me a minute to decide whether I wanted my mother to braid my hair.

All day yesterday with my hair down I had felt as if I had a wool scarf wrapped around my neck.

So which was better?

Feeling like I had a wool scarf around my neck?

Or wearing tight braids?

I set the empty glass on the counter by the sink and turned around.

"Was it hot upstairs last night?" Mom asked. She didn't wait for me to answer. "It must have been, if you're that thirsty."

"I guess you can braid my hair if you want to," I said.

"I really do think that would be best," Mom said. "Go get the brush and a couple of those hair bands your sister brought home for you."

I went into the bathroom for the brush and hair bands, set them on the table, and sat down on the floor in front of my mother. Mom lifted the hair off the back of my neck, and I braced myself for the first painful jolt. My hair was always snarly in the morning. Dad said I must stand on my head at night to get it so snarly.

I was still waiting for the first stab of pain when Mom drew a deep breath.

"Aye-yi-yi," she said. "You have one lovely heat rash."

"What's a heat rash?" I said.

"What it sounds like," Mom replied. "Your skin has a rash from the heat. Or maybe I should say it's from your hair holding the heat against the back of your neck."

"What does it look like?" I said.

"Little red dots," she replied. "Little red dots that probably itch."

I put my hand on the back of my neck. "No," I said. "It doesn't itch. But it does feel kind of sore."

"I'm going to have to be careful brushing," Mom said. "I don't want to scrape that rash and make it worse."

Much to my disbelief, for once, Mom took her time brushing my hair.

When she was finished, she divided my hair down the back.

"You know," she said, as she started to braid, "maybe you should get a haircut."

"A haircut? Why?" I said.

I had worn my hair short when I was a very little girl, but my hair had been long for the past couple of years.

"If you got a haircut, you wouldn't have any hair against your neck, and then that heat rash would go away," Mom replied.

She reached for one of the hair bands I had set on the table and wrapped it around the end of the braid. Then she started braiding the other half of my hair.

Not only had Mom gone slowly with the brush, but this was also the first time I could remember that she had not pulled the braids too tight.

"There, I'm done," Mom said after a while. "Think about the haircut. Okay?"

I stood up and turned toward her. "Okay," I said. "I'll think about it."

I put my barn shoes on and went outside. Usually the air felt cool first thing in the morning, but today, stepping outside was like standing next to the stove while Mom baked bread and boiled a kettle of potatoes and a kettle of sweet corn—all at the same time. Mom had been baking bread and boiling potatoes and sweet corn the other day, and Ingman said he was afraid to go in the kitchen because it was so hot, he thought he might melt.

I arrived in the barn a few minutes later just as Dad took the cover off a full milker bucket. Needles had stretched out on the barn floor not far away. The dog often stretched out on the cool concrete barn floor during the evening milking on hot days, but I had never seen him stretch out on the floor in the morning.

"What's wrong with Needles?" I asked.

At the sound of my voice, Needles opened his eyes, raised his head and thumped his tail against the floor.

Dad glanced at the dog. "Nothing is wrong with him. He's just hot." He turned to me. "I see you've got braids today."

"Mom said it would be better if it's going to be hot again."

"It'll be hot again, all right," Dad said.

I picked up the milker bucket and filled the stainless steel pail with milk. "Daddy?" I said as I set the milker bucket down. "Do you think I should get a haircut?"

"A haircut?" Dad said. "Why?"

"Because Mom says I've got a heat rash on the back of my neck, and that if I get my hair cut, I will feel cooler and the heat rash will go away."

"S'pose it might not be a bad idea," Dad said, grabbing the milker bucket with one hand and heading toward the next cow.

I picked up the stainless steel pail full of milk and carried it toward the door. I could lift a full milker bucket enough to fill the stainless steel pail, but I wasn't strong enough to carry a full milker bucket all the way to the milkhouse. The barn kitties, some trotting ahead of me, some behind me, and some next to me, ran to the cat dish. I stopped to fill their dish with fresh, warm milk, and then I carried the pail out into the early morning sunshine and headed for the milkhouse.

By the time the chores were finished and we had gone back to the house for breakfast, I had made up my mind. The back of my neck hadn't been itchy when I went out to the barn—but it sure was now.

"I think I should get a haircut," I said to Mom.

My mother stood by the counter, waiting for the toaster to launch the pieces of toast up into the air. Sometimes the toast jumped right out of the toaster. Dad said it was because the springs were too tight.

"What made you decide to get a haircut?" Mom asked.

"The back of my neck itches," I said. "It didn't itch when I went outside, but it does now.

"Maybe some cornstarch would help," Mom said. She reached up into the cupboard for the box of cornstarch, opened the cover and dipped two fingers inside.

"Turn around," she said

I turned my back to Mom, and I could feel her fingers stroking the cornstarch onto my neck.

"This will help keep it dry and maybe it will help keep it from getting worse," she said.

Mom put the cornstarch back in the cupboard. "I'm glad you decided to get your hair cut. I'll call and make an appointment for Saturday, and then Loretta can take you into town to the beauty shop."

The weather stayed hot and humid for the rest of the week, and by the time Saturday arrived, I could hardly wait to get all of that hot, itchy hair cut off.

The lady at the beauty shop worked on my hair for quite a long time. And as she snipped away with a small pair of scissors, I could hardly believe that all of the hair on the floor had come from my head.

No wonder my neck felt so hot and prickly.

With one final snip, the lady laid the scissors on the table in front of me, picked up a comb and ran it through my hair. She grasped the back of the chair and spun it around so that I was facing the mirror.

"What do you think?" she asked.

I stared at the person in the mirror who was staring back at me.

"It's so short!" I said.

"Well, yes, it is," Loretta said. "Is it too short?"

I stared at myself in the mirror some more and considered the question. Was my hair *too* short? But if it *was* too short, what difference would it make? I was pretty sure the lady at the beauty shop would not be able to glue it back on again.

And then I thought about my pony, Dusty, and how I had cut the burrs out of her mane and tail and forelock.

"I look like Dusty!" I said.

Loretta laughed. "Yes, you do. A little bit, I guess."

"Who is Dusty?" asked the lady.

My sister explained about my pony and how I had cut the burrs out of her mane and tail and forelock.

"Oh, I see," the lady replied.

Loretta paid for my haircut, and then we headed home. We drove the whole way with the windows rolled down in Loretta's green four-door Chevy Bel-Air. The wind blowing in the window felt strange on the back of my bare neck.

"Come in here so I can see," my mother said as soon as we walked into the kitchen.

Mom was in the living room, dusting the top of the little table by the east window where she kept her African violets.

"Oh, my," Mom said. "She cut it pretty short, didn't she."

"I think it's cute," Loretta said.

"Oh, yes, yes, it's cute," Mom said. "But it's very short."

A little while later, Dad and Ingman came in the house for dinner.

"Look at your hair!" Ingman said. "Or, what's left of it."

"Oh, jeepers, she cut it short," Dad said. "I didn't think she'd cut it *that* short."

"Don't you like it, Daddy?" I said.

My father shrugged. "I like it fine," he said. "You'll feel cooler and maybe you won't have that rash anymore, and that's the main thing."

Needles had come in the house with Dad and Ingman, as he always did at mealtime. But instead of sitting in his usual spot underneath the table by Dad's feet, he stretched out flat on the speckled linoleum, sides heaving as if he had run home from the other place.

"What's wrong with Needles?" Loretta asked.

"He's hot," Dad said. "It's awful humid outside, and I think that makes him feel hotter yet. He's got such thick hair, you know."

The dog's hair was so thick that whenever I soaked him with the hose from the milkhouse to give him a bath, I was always surprised by how small he looked with his hair plastered down.

When we had finished eating dinner, Dad and Ingman went outside. Needles went outside, too. But later on, when I went outside to see if Dad was doing anything interesting, I discovered that Needles had not gone far. He was stretched out north of the house, in the shade of the porch. Half his tongue hung out of his mouth, and as he panted, the end of his tongue dripped.

"Hi Needles," I said.

The dog lazily wagged his feathery tail.

"You're hot, aren't you," I said, crouching down beside him. He rolled over so I could scratch his belly.

"Poor, poor Needles. You must feel awful—"

And suddenly, as my hand petted the thick, heavy fur, I was struck by a brilliant idea.

I jumped to my feet. "Come on, Needles!"

The dog hopped up, shook himself, paused to stretch his front legs and then his back legs, and then he followed me to the barn.

In the barn, where it was dim and cool, Needles stood beside me, waiting patiently, while I took the cover off the twine barrel and reached down inside. The barrel had not been emptied for a long time, seeing as we didn't feed much hay in the summer. I pulled one string out of the barrel, looped it around Needle's collar, and tied him to a stall divider.

In the calf pen across the barn aisle, Crystal, the Angus mix calf, and another calf who had been born not long after watched me through the gaps in the boards.

"Maaaaa!" said Crystal.

"Hi, Crystal," I said.

I went to the corner by the calf pen and picked up the milk stool. I carried the stool across the barn aisle, set it on the floor near the milker pump, climbed up on it, stood on tiptoes and stretched as far as I could.

My arm was barely long enough to reach the scissors Dad kept hanging on a nail.

I climbed down off the stool and turned toward Needles.

"You're going to feel much better after this," I said.

Needles continued to watch me, ears perked, eyes bright, tail waving, tongue hanging out the side of his mouth. The calves watched me, too.

I slipped my fingers through the handle of the scissors and made the first snip in the skirts hanging from the back of Needles' legs. I knew that 'skirt' was not quite right, seeing as Needles was a boy, but I could think of no other way to describe the bushy hair hanging below his tail.

As Needles stood there patiently, I dropped the lock of thick, white hair onto the straw in the cow stall and made another snip. Soon, the bushy hair was gone from one hind leg, and in a few minutes, the bushy hair was gone from the other hind leg, too.

"Doesn't that feel better already, Needles?" I said.

"Maaaaaaa," said one of the calves in the pen.

Snip. Snip-snip. Snip.

A section of long hair from Needles' feathered tail dropped to the straw.

Snip. Snip. Snip.

Away went more of the hair from his tail.

When I had finished trimming his tail, I was amazed at how long and skinny it looked, more like a rope, actually, rather than the dog's tail.

"Now for the next part," I said, going after the long hair that grew from his belly.

Snip. Snip. Snip.

More white hair soon littered the straw.

Then I snipped off as much as I could from his chest.

After I was finished, I stood back to get a better look at Needles. In spite of his rope-like tail and the bare, ragged patches on his hind legs and belly and chest, I couldn't help feeling mighty pleased with myself.

"How's that?" I said as I untied the dog.

Realizing that he was free at last, Needles turned his head and sniffed his tail and the other places where he used to have long, cream-colored bushy hair. When he was finished looking at himself, he sniffed the white clumps scattered on the straw, his nose twitching from side to side as he carefully examined each little pile. Then he looked up at me and slowly wagged what was left of his tail.

As I admired my handiwork, I heard footsteps approaching on the driveway outside the barn.

"It's Dad!" I said. "Wait until he sees your haircut!"

My father walked into the barn and glanced at the dog. For a second, I thought he was going to keep walking, but he didn't. Instead, he stopped abruptly and turned toward us.

"What," he said, "have you done to Needles?"

"I gave him a haircut," I said, holding up the scissors, "so he would feel cooler."

I could not see my father's eyes very well because he was wearing his blue-and-white-pin-striped chore cap pulled down low on his forehead. But I *could* see that he had pursed his lips and had pressed them together. And I knew what that meant. It meant he was trying not to laugh out loud.

"Hah!" Dad said. His voiced sounded fuzzy, as if he had something caught in his throat. "Hah…hah-hah…a…haircut…a…hah!…a haircut…hah-hah!"

Needles, with ears and tail drooping, crept close to Dad and sat by his feet.

"Poor Needles," Dad said. He reached down and patted the top of the dog's head.

Poor Needles?

"What do you mean—'poor Needles?'" I said.

"He looks silly!" Dad exclaimed.

"He does *not* look silly," I retorted. "He feels cooler!"

"Well—maybe so. I guess there's nobody who knows how Needles feels except Needles himself," Dad said. "But he sure does look strange."

Needles, still sitting by Dad's feet, dropped his head lower and watched us from beneath eyebrows wrinkled into worry lines. I had seen Needles look like that once before when Mom yelled at him for making tracks on her freshly washed floor.

"What did I come in here for, anyway," Dad said. He lifted the cap off his head and settled it more firmly. "Oh, yes, that's right. I wanted some twine string to tie the granary door open."

Dad found the twine string he wanted and left the barn.

"You do not look silly, Needles," I said. "And you do not look strange. You look cooler! And when you go out to the field with Dad to cut some more hay, you'll feel cooler, too."

"Maaaaa!" said one of the calves.

Needles wagged only the very tip of his tail, and I noticed that the worry lines remained around his eyebrows.

I climbed on the milk stool and hung the scissors back on the nail.

"Come on, Needles," I said, when I had put the milkstool in the corner where it belonged. "Let's go show your haircut to Mom and Loretta."

I headed across the yard toward the house with Needles trotting at my heels.

"Come on, boy," I said, holding open the porch door." Here, Needles."

"Why are you bringing the dog in the house?" Mom asked. She stood in the living room doorway, the watering can for her African violets clutched in one hand.

"Yeeeek!" she said. "Needles! What *happened* to you?"

"What's wrong?" my sister's voice called out from upstairs. "What's wrong with Needles? Is he hurt?"

Loretta rushed down the steps and then stopped on the landing.

"Needles! What happened?" she said.

"Why," I said, as I flopped down on a kitchen chair, "does everyone keep asking what happened to Needles? Nothing 'happened' to him. I just gave him a haircut is all. So he would feel cooler."

My mother was curiously silent. I looked up and saw that her face had crumpled, that her eyes were squeezed shut and that she was trembling.

"Aggg-ha. Hah-hah-ah-hah," she said. She gave into it and opened her eyes. "Hah-hah-a…a…haircut!…ah-hah-ah-hah!"

At that moment, I realized Loretta was curiously silent, as well. She stood on the landing yet, and when I looked up at her, she had covered her mouth with one hand. She was trembling, too.

"Er-er-ah-ah,er-er," she said.

If I didn't know better, I would think she was crying.

Then she made the mistake of looking at Mom.

"Come on, Needles," I sat, jumping to my feet. "Let's go outside and find some shade."

As we left the house, I thought that maybe if I lived to be a thousand years old, I would never forget the sound of the shrieks, chortles and howls of laughter coming from the kitchen.

I crossed the yard with Needles right behind me and threw myself down on the cool, thick grass beneath the silver maples by Dusty's pasture. Needles laid down beside me. Minutes later, I heard the porch door slam and then the sound of rustling, swishing footsteps moving across the grass.

"I'm really sorry. We didn't mean to laugh," Loretta said, sitting down in the shade beside us.

"If you didn't mean to, then why did you?" I asked.

"Because, well, because it's funny," she said.

For some reason, my brother also had the same reaction when he saw Needles.

Personally, I didn't think it was one bit funny.

Needles didn't think it was especially funny, either. He skulked around for days after that, avoiding anyone who so much as smiled when they saw him.

It wasn't until everybody stopped laughing that Needles returned to his normal, cheerful self.

And then, so did I...

~ 17 ~
Enough is Enough

lip-clop-clip-clop went Dusty's hooves. The dew had not yet dried off the grass as the brown dappled pony and I made our way down the hill of the driveway. I knew as soon as the sun moved overhead, the grass would dry off, but right now, dew drops sparkled in the rays of sun glinting through the trees.

When we reached the end of the driveway, instead of turning left onto the road leading to our other place, we turned right. Dusty and I were going to see our next-door neighbor, Mrs. Paulson.

Mom did not want me to ride Dusty down to see Hannah too often because she was afraid the pony would eat Mrs. Paulson's flowers. Our next-door neighbor had planted petunias in big flowerpots, and she had planted zinnias and cosmos in her garden. Old-fashioned wild rose bushes grew next to the house, and so did clumps of wild spotted orange tiger lilies.

The lady who lived in the house before Hannah had transplanted the tiger lilies from where they grew wild in the ditches along the road.

For once I knew my mother was not going overboard and worrying too much. Dusty had a history of eating flowers. Not long ago, she had eaten half the petunias Loretta had planted around the yard light pole. I was sitting on her back, and I thought she was only eating grass *close* to the petunias. My mother had glanced out the kitchen window, saw that my pony was eating the flowers, and had let out a shriek that made Dusty pick up her head and look toward the house.

A few days later, I had ridden Dusty over to see Loretta, who was weeding a flowerbed she had planted in the middle of the lawn. My sister stood up to pet Dusty's neck, and the pony reached over and nipped off a clump of pink cosmos.

When the opportunity had presented itself, Dusty had eaten zinnias and marigolds, too. The marigolds must not have tasted too good because she had spit out some of the half-chewed up yellow blooms.

Dad said he wasn't surprised that Dusty liked to nip off flowers, seeing as she liked to nip people, too.

Almost from the day Dusty had come to live on our farm, she had liked to nip. She would pinch a person's skin between her front teeth, and although it couldn't exactly be called outright biting, it did hurt. At least that's what Dad and my big brother, Ingman, said. And Loretta, too. Dusty had nipped Loretta once while my sister petted the pony's neck. She nipped Ingman and Dad once or twice a week, Ingman more than Dad, though, because Ingman teased her about being a plump pony. I couldn't claim to know myself whether it hurt when Dusty nipped because for some reason, she had never nipped me.

As we passed the Paulson's bright-red barn, I reminded Dusty that she was not supposed to eat any flowers.

"If you eat Hannah's flowers, Mom will never *ever* let you come with me again," I said. "And you know what that means if you don't get to come down here."

We passed the milkhouse, and then we turned in on the front lawn where I could see Hannah next to the hedge, using what looked like a large pair of scissors. The giant scissors, I knew, was not a scissors at all, but was something called a hedge trimmer.

On top of her head, Hannah wore a wide-brimmed light blue straw hat tied beneath her chin with a blue and white flowered scarf. Her hands were covered by a pair of fuzzy yellow chore gloves with a red cuff, like the chore gloves Dad bought at the Farmer's Union in town. And she had tied a blue-and-white checkered apron over her pale yellow dress.

Mrs. Paulson was trimming the bottom part of the hedge. I nudged Dusty forward a few steps, and suddenly, my neighbor looked up and saw us.

"Well!" she said as she stood up straight, one hand on her lower back. "Look who's here!"

Dusty knew Mrs. Paulson was her friend. She practically trotted up to Hannah.

Mrs. Paulson smiled. "How are you, Dusty?"

The pony bobbed her head up and down, and Hannah nodded her head in return.

"I know you want," she said. "You want your treat. Wait right here."

Mrs. Paulson took of the chore gloves and laid them on the ground next to the hedge trimmers. As she made her way across the lawn toward the big, white house, I figured I had better get off and hold

Dusty's head. No flowers were growing nearby, but I wasn't going to take any chances.

A few minutes later, Hannah returned, and Dusty, who had been standing with one hind foot cocked, threw up her head and nickered.

Mrs. Paulson reached into the pocket of her apron and then held out her hand. Balanced on her palm was a single, white sugar cube.

Dusty took the sugar cube from her hand. *Crunch-crunch-crunch—* and then the sugar cube was gone.

"She makes quick work of a sugar cube, doesn't she," Hannah said as she reached into her pocket again.

"Dusty makes quick work of everything she eats," I said.

Once again, the pony took a sugar cube from Hannah's hand. And she kept right on taking the sugar cubes from Hannah until all six were gone.

Dusty did not get sugar cubes at home. Mom never bought them at the grocery store because no one in our family used sugar in their coffee.

Hannah held out her hands. "They're all gone, Dusty. See? My hands are empty."

Dusty nuzzled Hannah's fingers, and then she began to lick the palms of Mrs. Paulson's hands.

"All horses like sugar cubes, but you *really* like them," Mrs. Paulson said.

Dusty stopped licking Hannah's hands and looked at her steadily.

"I'm sorry, but that's all I brought, Dusty," Hannah said. "You probably shouldn't have too many, anyway. Wouldn't be good for your teeth. Besides, you're a rather plump little pony, and I don't think you need *too* many extra calories."

I had only begun to wonder why Dusty was looking at Mrs. Paulson like that when the pony thrust her nose forward. Before I could yell 'no!' and pull her back, she nipped Mrs. Paulson on the arm.

"Ouch!" Hannah cried, rubbing the spot where I could see tooth marks in her skin.

"Dusty!" I said, jerking back on the reins. "Shame on you!"

In an instant, I felt my throat growing tight, and I knew my face was turning red from my neck up to the tips of my ears.

Of all the embarrassing things that had ever happened to me— spilling a glass of milk on the table in front of Mom's cousin and his wife who had come for a visit—tripping and falling flat on my face when we were playing kickball at recess—forgetting to take the price tag off Loretta's Christmas present before I wrapped it—this was positively the worst. Mrs. Paulson was the nicest lady in the whole wide world. Next to my sister, of course.

"Dusty!" I said again. "Shame on you!"

And then hot tears spilled down my checks.

"There, there," Mrs. Paulson said. "Don't cry. You mustn't be angry with Dusty. She only wanted more sugar cubes."

"But she bit you!" I said.

"Well, yes," Hannah said, rubbing her arm, "she did."

"She bites Dad and Ingman, too," I said.

"She does?" Hannah said, looking at the pony.

I wiped the tears off my face. "Ingman more than Daddy. Ingman teases her about being plump."

Hannah reached up to adjust her wire-rimmed glasses. "Well, she *is* a plump little pony."

A short while later, as Dusty and I left Hannah's yard and headed for home, I wasn't quite sure which was worse: Dusty eating Mrs. Paulson's flowers—or Dusty biting Mrs. Paulson. Seeing as Dusty had not eaten any flowers, but she *had* nipped Hannah, I figured biting was worse.

And as we went up the hill toward our farm, it dawned on me that Dusty's nipping really was getting out of hand. I was afraid to tell Mom that Dusty had bitten Hannah, but I knew I was going to have to tell her, because if I didn't and Hannah mentioned it during one of their daily telephone calls, it would be that much worse.

But whether I told Mom or whether Hannah did, I knew my pony was never going to be allowed to visit Mrs. Paulson again.

With a slow *clip-clop-clip-clop—clip-clop-clip-clop,* Dusty climbed the hill. The sun was higher in the sky, and as we passed the front lawn, I could see that the dew had almost dried off the grass. I rode Dusty across the lawn to the little wooden gate in the corner of the yard and turned her loose in her pasture. Then I went back to the house.

"How is Hannah today?" Mom asked when I came into the living room. As she did most mornings, my mother sat in her chair by the living room window.

"Well, ummmm, she's all right. I guess."

Mom turned a steely blue gaze in my direction. "What's the matter?" she asked.

"Ummmm, well...you see..."

I stopped and swallowed. My throat suddenly felt as if it were filled with dry cotton balls.

"Well, ahh...errrr...Dusty bit Hannah," I said.

"What?" Mom said. "Dusty bit Mrs. Paulson? How *could* she? Did she break the skin?"

I shook my head. "No, Hannah wasn't bleeding. "

"Where did she bite her?"

"On the arm," I said. "After Hannah gave her some sugar cubes."

"Why...of all the ungrateful..."

"Hannah said Dusty just wanted more sugar cubes," I said.

"I don't care if Dusty wanted more sugar cubes," Mom said. "Shame on her."

My mother paused. "That's it. You are never taking that pony down there again. I was always afraid Dusty would eat Mrs. Paulson's flowers. But this is worse. Much worse."

"I know," I said.

"It's bad enough that she bites your father. And Ingman. And Loretta."

"I know," I said.

"I'm going to call Hannah and make sure she's all right," my mother said, reaching for the black telephone sitting next to her.

While my mother talked to Mrs. Paulson, I went outside, crossed the lawn and sat down in the swing hanging from one of the silver maples at the back of the yard. Dad had made the swing a few weeks ago, and I liked the swing on this side of the yard instead of on the clothesline. For one thing, the swing was in the shade here.

I pushed off, and as the swing moved back and forth, I could see my pony halfway down the hill in her pasture, picking grass, her white tail swishing from side to side. And all I could think about were the tooth marks on Hannah's arm.

If only I could find some way to convince Dusty that she shouldn't bite people.

The perfect opportunity, as it turned out, came along a few days later.

I often rode Dusty bareback in the summer. But today, I wanted to put the saddle on her. I kept the saddle and the rug and my brushes in the machine shed, and as I always did when I was going to put the saddle on, I tied Dusty to the door track.

I finished brushing the pony, went inside for the rug, came back out, laid it on her back, brought the saddle out and set it on top of the rug.

Just as I had done dozens of times before, I leaned over and reached underneath her belly to grab the girth. As I pulled the girth toward me, Dusty turned her head...

...and bit my arm.

I froze, my hand still on the girth, and the first thought that popped into my head was—'Dad and Ingman and Loretta and Hannah are right. It hurts!'

Seeing as I was bent over to reach for the girth, Dusty and I were nose to nose.

Before I even had time to think about it, I clamped my teeth onto the soft brown skin between Dusty's nostrils—and bit her back.

With a little squeal of surprise, Dusty jerked away and then stood there looking at me, blinking, as if she could not believe what had happened.

To tell you the truth, I wasn't sure *I* could believe it.

"See there, Dusty!" I said. "Doesn't feel so good, does it. You think it's so much fun to bite people, but I guess it's not so much fun if someone bites you."

I went around in front of her and tapped her on the nose. "Bad girl! You were very bad girl!" I said.

Dusty turned her head away from me, blinking from beneath the long white forelock that hung halfway down her forehead.

"What's all the commotion?" Dad asked.

I hadn't even realized my father was anywhere nearby. Dark spots dotted the front of his light blue chambray work shirt where water had splashed.

"I was in the milk house washing the bulk tank and heard you clear over there," he said.

"Dusty bit me!" I said.

"What?" Dad said.

"She bit me."

"Dusty! You didn't!" Dad said.

The pony still stared straight ahead.

"Where'd she get you?" he asked.

"On the arm," I said, turning my arm toward him where I could see tooth marks and a purple bruise beginning to show.

"Shame on you—you little rascal," he said.

"I bit her back," I said.

"You did what?"

"I bit her back."

"You bit her?"

"On the nose."

"On the nose?"

"I couldn't help it," I said. "I was reaching for the girth when she bit me, and well, her nose was right there. So I bit her back."

Dad grinned. "Maybe that'll teach you a lesson, Dusty."

I rubbed the spot on my arm where the pony had nipped me.

"Does it hurt?" Dad asked.

"Kinda," I said.

"She's got a good way of getting your skin between her teeth, I can say that much for her," Dad said.

"Yes," I said. "She does."

"Well," Dad said, "if that's all that's wrong, I'm going back to finish the bulk tank."

He turned and headed for the milkhouse.

Cautiously, I leaned over and reached for the girth again. But Dusty still stared straight ahead and for the rest of the time that it took to put on the saddle, the pony never so much as looked at me.

When several weeks had gone by and Dusty had not bitten anyone, Dad mentioned it at supper one night.

"You know, I gave Dusty the perfect opportunity to bite me today, but she didn't even act like she wanted to," he said as he buttered a slice of bread.

"What were you doing?" Mom asked.

"Pounding in a staple on the fence by the gate," Dad replied. "She was standing right there, by my elbow. But now that I think about it, she hasn't tried to bite me in a long time."

My brother reached for his glass of milk. "Hmmmmm," Ingman said, "and she hasn't bitten me in a long time, now that you mention it."

"Or me," Loretta said. "Of course, she only bit me that one time. But once was enough!"

"You don't suppose she's gotten over her bad habit of biting, do you," Mom said.

"Could be," Dad said. He turned his head toward me and his right eye closed in a wink.

"What are you winking about?" Mom asked.

"Didn't the kiddo tell you?" Dad said.

My mother frowned. "Tell me what?"

"What?" Loretta said.

"What?" Ingman asked.

"You'd better tell them," Dad said.

I drew a deep breath and let it out slowly.

"Dusty bit me," I said.

"She did!" Mom said.

"That little stinker!" Loretta said.

"Really?" Ingman said.

"So I bit her back," I said.

Mom, Loretta and Ingman stared at me, eyebrows raised high on their foreheads.

"You did *what*?" Mom said.

"I bit her back," I said. "On the nose."

"On the nose?" Mom said.

"Well," Loretta said. "Maybe Dusty learned her lesson!"

"I hope so," Ingman said. "It hurts when she bites!"

"Sure does," Dad said.

I looked down at the flowered oilskin tablecloth for a moment.

"Mom," I said, "if it's true that Dusty doesn't bite anymore, can I—I mean—may I ride her down to see Hannah?"

My mother frowned as she considered the question. "Well, once you're sure she has stopped biting, yes, you may ride her down to see Hannah, just as long as you promise to watch her so she doesn't eat any flowers."

"I promise!" I said.

For a long time after that, I waited to see if Dusty would bite somebody else. But she never did.

Then again, I never bit anyone else after that, either.

****

~ 18 ~
The Grass is Always Greener

I opened my eyes. What was that strange noise? It almost sounded like something…ringing. Wait a minute. It *was* something ringing. I pulled my hand from beneath the sheet and reached over to shut off the alarm clock. It was a travel alarm, and the case was the color of the hard butterscotch candies that came wrapped in matching cellophane. The clock belonged to my big sister, Loretta, but she hardly ever used it.

When I had finally shut off the alarm, I flipped back the covers and sat up. How could it be 6:30 already? Feeling as if I had only gone to sleep a few minutes ago, I pulled on a pair of shorts and a t-shirt. Through the open upstairs window I could hear Dad calling the cows. During the summer, I often awoke to the sound of 'come-boss, come-boss.'

As I pushed my hands into my pockets to straighten out the liners, the sound of the last 'come-boss' died away in the cool morning air. I knew that any second now, Dad would call 'come-boss' again. And that he would keep calling the cows until all of them were headed toward the barn.

Except that today Dad did not call 'come-boss' again.

Instead I heard—"Get outta here! Whatsa matter with you?"

I looked out the window. Some of the cows stood in the lane and some stood just inside the barnyard gate.

If the cows were in the lane and in the barnyard, why was Dad yelling at them?

Suddenly, a cow appeared from between the rows of tall green corn growing in the field next to the barnyard. And right then and there, I knew why my father was yelling at the cows.

The cows were out in the corn again.

For the third time.

I hurried downstairs.

"The cows are out in the corn!" I said.

"I know," my mother replied. "I've been watching Dad trying to get them back in the barnyard. I thought about waking you up, but I knew you'd be coming downstairs soon enough, anyway."

I went out to the porch, grabbed my shoes and put them on. Then I pushed open the door, leaped down the porch steps and trotted toward the barn.

When I crawled through the fence, the cows in the lane turned their heads to watch me. They were used to seeing people crawl through fences, and only one of the Holsteins snorted and shook her head before backing away a few steps.

"Get outta here!" Dad said. He took off his chore cap and waved it at a Holstein heifer who was chewing on a stalk of corn.

"What should I do, Daddy?" I said.

My father put the cap back on his head. "Good. I'm glad you're here. Go in the barn and put the feed in. And then let the rest of the cows inside. If they see the other cows going in, maybe they'll want to go in, too."

"How many are in the corn?" I asked.

"Same as before. Six. The two heifers and four of the younger cows. Now go put the feed in."

"Yes, Daddy," I said.

A short while later, I had put feed in the mangers in front of the stanchions, and I was on my way down the barn aisle to open the door. One by one, the cows rushed into the barn. *Clickety-clack, clickety - clack* went their hooves on the concrete floor, and as they began to eat their feed, I went around shutting stanchions. When the last of them had come inside, I walked out to the barnyard.

"Would you open the gate?" Dad said. "I shut it so the rest of them wouldn't take advantage of it."

Although the four strand barb wire gate usually was tight and hard for me to open, now it seemed loose and sloppy.

"What happened to the gate?" I said.

"That's how they got in here," Dad replied. "I think one of those heifers must have figured out how to knock it down. I shut it again to keep the rest of the cows out."

I opened the gate, pulled it back, and propped the post against the fence.

"I'll see if I can chase one out, and when I do, shut the gate behind us," he said.

The sun had moved high enough in the sky to shine through the trees along the fence by Dusty's pasture. Dewdrops sparkled on the grass, and barn swallows chattered as they flew over the corn, looking for bugs. Corn leaves rustled in the slight breeze, but from farther away came the sound of corn stalks snapping and cracking as Dad tried to chase the cows out of the field. And even though the morning air was still cool, I could smell the corn, a sweet scent that was a little like vanilla.

In a few minutes, Dad managed to chase one of the cows out of the cornfield. I closed the gate and then waited for him to bring the next cow out—and then the next—and the next. Eventually all six of them stood in the barnyard.

"Come-bossie," Dad said. "Come-bossie, come-bossie."

The two heifers and the four cows followed him into the barn.

"Daddy?" I said.

"What kiddo," he replied as he closed the first stanchion.

"How come the other cows didn't go through the gate, too, and get into the cornfield?"

"I don't know," Dad said. "Maybe they didn't realize the gate was open."

He went to the next stanchion. "Good thing, too," he said. "I'd hate to try to chase 'em all out of the corn."

Dad finished closing the stanchions and headed toward the other end of the aisle. "Well, now that the cows are all in barn," he said, "I suppose we can start milking."

After that, the morning milking went as usual, and an hour later, we were ready to go into the house for breakfast.

"How did the cows get into the cornfield?" Mom asked.

"Knocked the gate down," Dad said.

"Did they do a lot of damage?" Mom asked.

"Some," Dad said. "They broke off corn along the end by the gate."

"How are you going to keep them out?" she asked. "This is the third time!"

"I think I'm going to have to string an electric fence," Dad said.

"Been a long time since we've had an electric fence," Mom said.

"I'd just as soon not put up an electric fence," Dad said, "but I don't want 'em in the corn again, either. When I'm done with the milkers, I guess I'll have to go to town and buy a battery for the fencer."

"Will they get in the corn again while you're gone?" Mom asked.

"Probably not," Dad said. "I think they make trouble when they're standing around waiting to come in the barn in the morning. They can't possibly be hungry. Not with all the pasture they've got."

"Well," Mom said. "You know what they say, 'the grass is always greener on the other side of the fence.'"

I looked at my mother. "But, Mom. There isn't any grass on the other side of the fence. It's corn!"

"I know," Mom said. "It's a saying. It means that what you don't have looks better than what you do have."

I thought about this for a bit.

"Is that why Dusty pokes her head through the fence into the cow pasture," I said, "to eat the grass that's there rather than eating what's in her pasture?"

"Yup," Dad said. "Same kind of grass, but because it's on the other side of the fence, she thinks it's better."

After we had eaten breakfast, Dad and I went back to the barn. We let the cows out, and then, while my father washed the milkers, I swept the barn aisle and the mangers and sprinkled white barn lime on the floor. The smell of the barn lime reminded me of the chalk dust at school when we cleaned the erasers. I would rather not think about school starting, even though it was still a few weeks away.

I had almost finished sprinkling lime when Dad came in the barn.

"You wanna go to town with me, kiddo?" he asked. "Now that I'm done with the milkers, I've got to go to the Farmers' Union to get a battery for the fencer. Probably ought to get some insulators, too."

"Could I?"

"Sure," he replied, "but we'd better find out if Ma wants anything from town first. Run in the house and ask, and I'll bring the pickup around."

By the time I came out of the house, Dad had parked the truck by the little pump house next to the garage.

"Does Ma want anything?" he asked as I opened the door.

"Shortening," I said. "Loretta would like to make some pies out of those peaches you bought the other day, but Mom said she doesn't think she has enough shortening."

Dad had bought two lugs of peaches at the grocery store a few days ago. Every summer we ended up with a couple of lugs of peaches. Mom wanted to can some of them and make peach sauce. Loretta said she would make peach pie. The rest we would eat fresh. I thought it was strange that boxes of peaches were called 'lugs' but that's what Mom and Dad called them.

"Mmmm," Dad said. "Peach pie sounds good. Do you what *kind* of shortening we're supposed to get?"

"Yes," I said. "I know what kind."

"Good," he said. "Because I wouldn't have any idea."

My father started to turn the key in the ignition and then stopped. Our dog, Needles, stood in the driveway looking at the pickup truck with sad brown eyes.

"Should we let Needles come with us, too?" Dad asked. "We're not going to the feed mill."

Ever since Needles had growled at one of the guys at the feed mill when he had tried to get in the truck to move it, Dad had figured the dog should stay home. But we weren't going to the feed mill today.

I opened my door. "Come here, Needles!" I said.

The dog took one look at me, gathered himself, and leaped into the truck. His fur tickled the backs of my bare legs as he scooted underneath. He crawled up on the seat between Dad and me, turned around and sat down, panting happily. He looked for all the world like he was smiling.

"Didn't take you long to get in, did it," Dad said.

As my father started the truck, I put my arm around Needles. He turned his head and licked my face until I thought I wouldn't have any skin left on that part of my cheek. Going to town with Dad was fun, but when Needles came with us, it was twice as much fun.

When we arrived in town, Dad parked along the street by the Farmer's Union. We rolled the windows down an inch or two so Needles could get some fresh air. Inside the Farmers' Union, Dad bought a battery for the fencer and some insulators for the little electric fence posts. The fence posts looked like metal sticks with a triangle at the bottom. I had asked Dad once what the triangle was for, and he said it was meant to help keep the post in the ground.

After Dad had paid for his purchases, we put the battery and the insulators in the truck, and then we walked down the street to the grocery store.

My father and I had found the shortening, and I had no more than pointed out which one we were supposed to get, when a voice spoke up behind me.

"Guess what we're going to do tomorrow?!"

I turned around. It was one of the girls from my class at school who lived in town. Her mother stood behind her.

"What are you going to do tomorrow?" Dad replied.

"We're going swimming. And we're taking a picnic! It's going to be a beach party! All the girls who live in town are coming to my party!"

I had seen the girl's mother a couple of times at school.

The woman smiled at me. "Say! Would like you to come, too? There's always room for one more. We're just going to the park here in town. I haven't decided about the swimming yet."

The idea of a picnic sounded like a whole lot of fun. During the summer, I hardly ever saw any of the other kids from my class, unless I ran into them at the grocery store or the hardware store or at the fair in June. But June seemed like a long time ago now.

I turned toward Dad with an eager smile—but the smile died away when I saw that he was shaking his head.

"We've got to bale that field of hay tomorrow. Ingman will be working, and I was thinking you could drive the four-sixty," he said.

The woman smiled again. "Well," she said, "maybe some other time, then."

They were halfway down the grocery store aisle when I heard the girl speak up. "Boy, I sure am glad *we* don't live on a farm," she said. "I would rather go on picnics than to be stuck out in the country on some dumb, old farm."

The woman glanced back at us. I quickly turned toward the shelf and reached for the can of shortening.

A little while later on the way home, it seemed to me that going to town with Dad and Needles hadn't been *quite* as much fun as I thought it would be.

"You take the shortening in the house," Dad said as he parked the truck under the silver maple by the gas barrel. "I'm going to see if the fencer still works. Then I'll get the posts and insulators ready. And then I'll come in the house for dinner."

"Okay, Daddy," I said.

"And after dinner, maybe you could help me put in the posts and string that wire. It'll go quicker with two of us," he said.

"Okay," I said.

A minute later, I set the paper bag with the can of shortening on the kitchen table.

"Mom? How come we can't live in town?"

My mother was sitting by the table cutting up leftover roast and cold potatoes to make hash for dinner.

"What?" she said.

"How come we can't live in town?"

"Why would you want to live in town?" she asked.

She frowned and looked at me closely. "Well," she said. "Sure. We *could* sell the farm. And your dad could get a job somewhere. And we could buy a house in town."

"Really?" I said.

She nodded. "Of course we could. So what brought that up?"

I sat down on a kitchen chair. "I saw one of the girls from my class in the grocery store. She's having a beach party tomorrow. And her mom asked if I wanted to come. But Daddy said we have to bale hay."

"Oh," Mom said.

"I *never* get to do anything fun!" I wailed. "The girls who live in town *always* get to do something fun! And I have to bale hay! It's not fair!"

"I see," Mom said. She paused and cut up another cold potato.

"You do realize," she continued, "that if we sell the farm and move to town, you would have to sell Dusty."

I turned to look at her. "Sell Dusty?"

"Yes, you would have to sell Dusty," she said.

A cold fear clutched at my heart. "But why?" I said.

"You can't keep a pony in town," Mom said. "They have laws about such things. Plus, we wouldn't have a barn. Or a pasture. So you'd have to sell her if we moved to town. And you'd have to give Needles away, too."

"Give Needles away? But other people keep dogs in town," I said.

She reached for another potato. "It wouldn't be fair to Needles. He would have to be tied up because he isn't used to being in town. But you wouldn't want him to be tied up all of the time, would you? Except that if he wasn't tied up, he might wander out in the street and get run over."

My mother finished cutting the potato into chunks.

"And we'd have to leave all of the barn cats here, too," she said.

"We would?"

"Of course," she said, reaching for another potato. "We wouldn't have a barn, so where would the kitties live? They wouldn't have any place for their kittens."

She started cutting the potato.

"And it goes without saying," my mother continued, "that we would either have to sell the cows or else leave them here for whoever bought the farm."

She stopped cutting the potato and looked at me.

"And we'd have to give your toboggan away, too," she said.

"My toboggan?" I said.

"There's no place in town to go with a toboggan," she said as she started cutting the potato again. "Just by Mirror Lake, but it's usually full of people skating in the winter, so that wouldn't work very well."

I stared at my mother, unable to believe what I had just heard. Dusty? Needles? The barn cats? The cows? *And* my toboggan?

Soon my mother had finished cutting up the potatoes.

"Would you go out to the garden and get an onion for me?" she asked.

I went to the garden to fetch an onion so Mom could chop it up and put it in the hash.

After a while, Dad came in for dinner, and when we were finished eating, it was time to put up the electric fence. Between the two of us, the work went quickly, and an hour later, an electric fence was strung along the lane and the pasture and by the gate. My father turned on the fencer. *Click-clock, click-clock, click-clock, click-clock* said the little red box that held the battery.

"Whatever you do, don't touch that wire. You'll get a shock," Dad said.

I looked at the cows, who had come to the barnyard when we were partway through putting up the fence.

"But won't the cows get a shock, too?" I asked.

My father nodded. "That's the general idea," he said.

One of the heifers approached the wire, touched it with her nose, and then, with a loud snort, jumped back and ran to the other side of the barnyard.

"Hah!" Dad said. "Remember that. *And stay away from my cornfield.*"

A couple of the other cows came up to the electric fence and touched it with their noses, too—and had the same reaction as the heifer.

"Yup. I think it's going to work fine," Dad said.

He turned to me. "Why don't you go and get Dusty and ride her along the fence by the Bluff and see if there's any ripe blackberries. If there is, we can pick some tomorrow morning while we're waiting for the dew to dry off so we can bale."

"Do you think there's any ripe?" I said.

"Ought to be at least few," he replied. "We probably won't have a real big crop this year. It was too dry earlier this summer. But maybe there's enough for a pie. And for a couple of pints of jam."

"And for blackberries and cream?" I said.

"Maybe," Dad said. He turned to pick up the tools he had used for the electric fence.

"Daddy? Do people who live in town get to pick blackberries?" I asked.

My father shook his head. "Not in town, they don't. Blackberries don't grow in town. If they want blackberries, they have to go out to somebody's farm."

"Blackberries don't grow in town?"

"Nope. If they want blackberries, they have to go to a farm," Dad said. "That's if they know anybody who's got a farm who will let 'em pick berries."

Now here was something I hadn't thought about before.

Blackberries don't grow in town.

I crawled through the fence and crossed the lawn. Dusty was grazing in the shade of the silver maples on the sidehill below the house.

"Hi, Dusty," I said.

The pony threw her head up, nickered, walked a few steps and then broke into a fast trot. She stopped when she was a few feet away, and with her soft brown nose, reached up to nuzzle my hair.

"That tickles," I said.

I took hold of the pony's halter and led her to the gate where Dad waited with my rope reins dangling from one calloused, work-roughened hand. He gave the reins to me so I could clip them onto Dusty's halter.

"What's the cement block for?" I asked.

A cement block sat on the ground near the gate.

"I thought you could hop up on that to get on Dusty instead of going all the way around to the granary step," Dad said.

While Dad opened the gate, I got on Dusty, and a minute later, we were riding across the pasture toward the Bluff.

Needles, who had been sleeping in the shade of the barn while we put up the electric fence, trotted along beside us. The motion of Dusty's walk was like sitting in a rocking chair.

As we came closer to the fence next to the Bluff, I began to look at the blackberry briars. The brambles along the fence were as tall as me, but as far as I could tell, they did not have any berries.

No, wait. There was a berry.

And another one.

And another one.

And as we went farther along the fence, I saw handfuls of black, shiny, juicy berries.

Maybe enough berries for pie. And for jam. And for blackberries and cream.

Dusty and I rode to the corner of the pasture where there were brown-eyed Susans blooming and lacy white flowers that our neighbor, Hannah, called yarrow. The white flowers with their frilly green leaves smelled spicy, like a cross between peppermint and a pine tree.

The pony and I turned around and started back while Needles snuffled in the long grass by the fence. A rabbit ran out, and the dog chased it across the field until he saw he would not be able to keep up with it. Then he stopped and came back.

Knowing that we were headed toward the barn, Dusty broke into a trot. And as we jogged along in the bright afternoon sunshine, I began to snicker.

The snickers soon turned into giggles, and by the time we reached the gate, I was laughing so hard I could barely catch my breath. I slid off the pony, put my arms around her neck and buried my face in her thick, white mane. I stood there until I could breathe again, drawing in the smell of horse sweat and green grass.

And as I turned to open the gate—that's when it hit me.

How could I have ever thought I'd want to live anywhere else but on a farm?

~ Acknowledgements ~

Thank you to my husband, Randy Simpson, who, after four books, still says he's my biggest fan. Randy also is my website designer, my business partner, my administrative assistant, my book cover designer—and the person who tells me to keep going on those days when I feel like giving up.

And—like I always say—thank you to my readers, because without readers, writers wouldn't have a job!

****

~ How to Order More Books ~

Here's how to order more copies of *Where the Green Grass Grows*, *Cream of the Crop*, *Give Me a Home Where the Dairy Cows Roam* and *Christmas in Dairyland:*

• Order on the Internet through Booklocker.com
• Order on the Internet through Amazon.com or Barnes & Noble.
• Order through your local bookstore.
• Call LeAnn at (715) 962-3368.
• Write to LeAnn at E6689 970th Ave.; Colfax, WI 54730
• Order from LeAnn's website—www.ruralroute2.com

When you order books directly from the author (either by calling, writing or ordering through www.ruralroute2.com), you can request autographed copies with personalized inscriptions. And no need to pre-pay. An invoice will be sent with your order. Free shipping!

****

~ Book Review ~

Give Me a Home Where the Dairy Cows Roam
(Oct. 2004; ISBN-1-59113-592-3; $13.95; www.ruralroute2.com)

Give Me A Home Where The Dairy Cows Roam is a collection of autobiographical stories drawn from author LeAnn Ralph's family dairy farm in Wisconsin in a time when small family farms were commonplace in the Badger State's rural countryside.

Now that we live in a time when approximately 85% of American family dairy farms have disappeared into suburban township developments or absorbed into agribusiness scale corporate farming enclaves, LeAnn takes us back some forty years ago into an era when dairy farming was a dawn-to-dusk life, seven days a week lifestyle that bonded parents and children with hard work and a sense of the land, animals, and homestead that is rapidly passing from today's expanding urban society.

More than just an autobiographical collection of anecdotal stories, *Give Me A Home Where The Dairy Cows Roam* is also enhanced with a recipe for making homemade ice cream without an ice cream maker and a recipe for "Norma's Homemade Bread". Highly recommended reading, *Give Me A Home Where The Dairy Cows Roam* should be on the shelves of every community library in Wisconsin.

James A. Cox, Editor-in-Chief
Midwest Book Review

****

~ Book Review ~

Christmas in Dairyland (True Stories from a Wisconsin Farm)
(August 2003; ISBN 1-59113-366-1; $13.95; www.ruralroute2.com)

Christmas In Dairyland: True Stories From A Wisconsin Farm by LeAnn R. Ralph is a heartwarming anthology of true anecdotes of rural life on a Wisconsin dairy farm. Even though Wisconsin is still known as America's Dairyland, life on a family homestead is fast being replaced by corporate agribusiness, and the memories treasured in *Christmas In Dairyland* are quickly becoming unique milestones of an era needing to be preserved in thought and print for the sake of future generations. *Christmas In Dairyland* is simply wonderful reading and is a "must" for all Wisconsin public library collections.

James A. Cox, Editor-in-Chief
Midwest Book Review

****

~ Book Review ~

Cream Of The Crop: More True Stories Form A Wisconsin Farm
(October 2005; ISBN 1591138205; $13.95; www.ruralroute2.com)

Cream of the Crop is the third anthology of biographical and anecdotal stories by LeAnn Ralph about growing up on a Wisconsin dairy farm. In the 1960s there were more than 60,000 dairy farms in Wisconsin, in May of 2004 the Wisconsin Agricultural Statistics Service recorded the number of surviving dairy farms in the state at 15,591. The number has dropped even lower since then. That dairy farming reality is what helps to give LeAnn's deftly told stories their nostalgia for a rural lifestyle that is not-so-slowly disappearing in the Badger state. There are twenty short but immensely entertaining stories in this simply superb anthology. They range from "What's in a Name", to "She'll Be Comin' Round the Cornfield", to "Gertrude and Heathcliff", to the title story "Cream Of The Crop". LeAnn continues to write with a remarkable knack for making people and events come alive in the reader's imagination. Also very highly recommended are LeAnn's two earlier anthologies about life on the family farm in Wisconsin: *Give Me A Home Where The Dairy Cows Roam* (1591135923, $13.95) and *Christmas In Dairyland: True Stories From A Wisconsin Farm* (1591133661, $13.95).

James A. Cox, Editor-in-Chief
Midwest Book Review

****

~ About the Author ~

LeAnn R. Ralph earned an undergraduate degree in English with a writing emphasis from the University of Wisconsin-Whitewater and also earned a Master of Arts in Teaching from UW-Whitewater. She has worked as a newspaper reporter for nearly 10 years all together, has taught English at a boys' boarding school, has worked as a substitute teacher and a parish secretary, and is the former editor of the *Wisconsin Regional Writer* (the quarterly publication of the Wisconsin Regional Writers' Assoc.).

The author lives in rural Wisconsin with her husband, two dogs, two horses and assorted cats. She is working on her next book, *The Coldest Day of the Year*, another collection of true stories.

If you would like to find out when LeAnn's next book is available, write to her at E6689 970th Ave., Colfax, WI 54730, or e-mail her at — bigpines@ruralroute2.com

Besides *Where the Green Grass Grows*, LeAnn is the author of the books, *Cream of the Crop* (trade paperback; September 2005; $13.95) *Give Me a Home Where the Dairy Cows Roam* (trade paperback; September 2004; $13.95); *Christmas in Dairyland (True Stories from a Wisconsin Farm)* (trade paperback; August 2003; $13.95) and *Preserve Your Family History (A Step-by-Step Guide for Writing Oral Histories)* (e-book; April 2004; $7.95).

****

~ About the Book Cover ~

The black Holstein calf was photographed on the front lawn of our farm. Below the hill, you can see our next-door neighbor's place. Dusty's pasture is behind the trees at the edge of the lawn.

The calf was the daughter of a Holstein we called Smoothie. The mother was shiny black and so smooth to the touch. We called the calf—what else?—Baby.

****